American

Typography

Today

American

Typography

Today

VNR Van Nostrand Reinhold
_____ New York

Rob Carter

Copyright © 1993 by Van Nostrand Reinhold

Library of Congress Catalog Card Number 88-21616
ISBN 0-442-22106-1
ISBN 0-442-01457-0 (paperback)

Printed in the United States of America

Van Nostrand Reinhold
115 Fifth Avenue
New York, New York 10003

Chapman and Hall
2-6 Boundary Row
London SE1 8HN, England

Thomas Nelson Australia
102 Dodds Street
South Melbourne 3205
Victoria, Australia

Nelson Canada
1120 Birchmount Road
Scarborough, Ontario M1K 5G4, Canada

16 15 14 13 12 11 10 9 8 7 6 5 4 3 2 1

Library of Congress Cataloging-In-Publication Data

Carter, Rob.
        American Typography Today / Rob Carter.
        p.   cm.
        Bibliography: p.
        Includes index.
        ISBN 0-442-22106-1
        ISBN 0-442-01457-0 (paperback)
1. Printing—United States—History—20th century.   2. Book
design—United States—History—20th century.   3. Type and type-
founding—United States—History—20th century.   I. Title.

        Z208.C37 1989   88-21616
        686.2'2'0973—dc19   CIP

For my children:

Molly Ann Carter, Mindy Dawn Carter, and Jed Robert Carter

Contents

Foreword

Two decades ago, the oracles of the approaching electronic age declared that Gutenberg's galaxy would soon collapse, consumed by the immediacy of television and other electronic media. Some even suggested that traditional literacy skills were becoming irrelevant, for telethis and telethat, push-button electronic banking, and a host of other wonders would allow citizens to dispense with such inane skills as reading, and arithmetic would be out of date. Today we find that the electronic age has increased, rather than diminished, our need for typographic literacy. The noble art of typography has been extended electronically in time and space, has undergone an unprecedented explosion of technology and new styles, and has been renewed by the amazing creativity of designers.

In writing this book, Rob Carter set out to capture the current state of American typographic design. Two dozen masters of contemporary typography are presented through portfolios of their work and insightful critical evaluations. A timeline of events and a compelling list of resources—a little *Whole Earth Catalog* of designers, movements, and philosophers that have shaped contemporary typographic thought— round out the volume.

Carter's selection of 24 designers was made over a two-year period by carefully studying and evaluating the spectrum of contemporary practice. He gives us a cross-section of major directions, including the formal rigor of modernism, the playful and expressive manifestations of post-modernism, revivals of classic form, avant-garde experiments, and explorations of language, sign, and symbol. A geographic and philosophic balance was sought. A list of over 100 potential candidates for this book was painstakingly reduced to 50, then 30, persons. Production limitations required further tightening to the 24 persons presented here. Certainly, everyone involved in contemporary typography will miss some of their favorite designers. My list, for example, would have included the objective design of Rudy De Harak and William Longhauser's innovative post-modernism. Even so, Carter's selection of designers and their work is impeccable. His clarity of writing and keen insights about design provide an invaluable understanding of American typography.

The stunning design of this book becomes an appropriate vehicle for its contents; one of those rare occasions when the vessel and contents are fully worthy of each other. As a designer, writer, and teacher, Rob Carter has an unending love for typography and design. We are indeed fortunate that he has undertaken the complex task of compiling and writing this book.

Philip B. Meggs

Acknowledgments

Many thanks go to the featured designers; their contributions to the profession made this book possible.

I would also like to thank the following people: Murry N. DePillars and John DeMao, for continuous encouragement and support; my colleagues and friends, Philip B. Meggs and Ben Day, for enthusiastically and regularly giving direction about content and for sharing their expertise in the areas of design history and theory; Dolly Plumb, Diana Lively, John Bryan, Tina Brubaker Chovanec, and Steve Chovanec, for reading various stages of the manuscript and providing valuable criticism; Keith Jones, for generously sharing research materials; Joshua and Phyllis Heller for sharing their valuable time, resources, and ideas; and my wife, Sally Carter, for serving as a sounding board and for her unfailing patience.

Lilly Kaufman, Sponsoring Editor at Van Nostrand Reinhold, provided encouragement and direction throughout the project, for which I am grateful; Brooks Donnelly, Editorial Supervisor, provided immeasurable editorial support; and Sandra Cohen, Production Manager, provided invaluable skill and attention in bringing the project to fruition.

Thanks to George Nan, for his impeccable photography and for his willingness always to take "just one more shot"; to Mark Uskavitch, for creating the computer-generated pattern that is integral to the design of the book; and to Jerry Bates and staff, for graphic arts assistance.

Introduction

During the early part of the twentieth century, restless European artists reacted vigorously to the social changes accompanying the industrial revolution. They reassessed the human condition, concluding that the traditions of the past no longer met the needs of the modern world. It was a time of rejection and reformation, and of moving forward. The soul of the machine was embraced by these pioneers of the modern movement and reflected in their art and design.

•

Cubism was the first of a long line of "isms" to express discontent, followed by Futurism, Dadaism, Surrealism, and Constructivism. These were outspoken movements that greatly altered the course of typographic development. Filippo Marinetti for example, the founder of Futurism, launched an unprecedented typographical revolution that imposed total velocity upon words—"that of the stars, of the clouds, of the airplanes, of the trains, of the waves, of the explosives. . . ."

•

Attitudes about typography changed drastically during these years, forcing acceptance of possibilities denied for centuries. Poets and artists used typography not only as something to be read, but also as something to be seen— as a carrier of visual messages. In other words, its very appearance could affect the meaning of a message. Dissident typographic manipulations brought exasperated sighs from traditionalists as letters were abruptly pulled from the safety of their horizontal orientation.

•

The practitioners of this new typography differed philosophically, but on one point they all agreed: art and design must embody the spirit of the times. For them, the purely linear approach to typography was a limitation to be reckoned with, for it encouraged linear thinking as well. Only by removing the barrier between typographic form and content, and by destroying traditional syntax, could this dilemma be resolved.

•

America was slow in accepting the tenets of Modernism. Graphic design and typography in the early part of the century reflected the commonplace sentimentality of the nin century. It was not until the 1930s th Modernism did gain a foothold. Some greatest cultural minds of Europe, in Fascism, moved to America, bringing ideas with them. The enormous influe of their presence has been felt for sever

•

The 1930s and 1940s were a time of synthesis. American designers applied transplanted European vocabulary to design. By the 1950s, two major dir evolved: the highly eclectic American of Graphic Expressionism and the objec International Typographic Style.

•

The late 1970s marked the advent o modernism in American graphic des that the modern aesthetic no longer held relevance in post-industrial society, prac (primarily of the International Typograp Style) began to broaden their visual voca by breaking established rules and by various periods, styles, and cultures.

•

During the 1980s, the pluralistic nat American graphic design has become evident. While the Neoclassicists have busy restoring old values, "New Wave have been busy tearing them down. The "Eclectic Expressionists" borrow freely from available sources. With more stylistic persu sions now characterizing American typograph than ever before, it is easy to understand why typographic tastes have become even mo fickle than fashion tastes.

•

The wide range of influences in American typographic design leads to basic concerns. Whi eclecticism can propel designers into a search for individuality and innovative thinking, blin historicism can threaten the integrity of design's uncompromising purpose: to appropriately solv communication problems. When influences of the past are applied without a concern for relevant context, they are reduced to gimmic and tricks. But when designers understand that typography is a language possessing a specific syntax and grammar of form, capable

' (visual) and "symbolic" (verbal)
influences may enhance the crea-
    as long as they are viewed in
 text.

 ry aim of *American Typography Today*
   the current state of American
   design by providing readers with a
   of design approaches. This is
 d by presenting profiles of notable
   designers (Part 1), and by surveying
 urces of twentieth-century typography
 n addition, a selective chronology
 ive American typographic designers
   '940 is illustrated.

 selecting a balanced yet diverse
 esigners for the profiles section was a
 one, requiring the use of carefully
 riteria: stylistic, philosophic, and geo-
 balance was the primary requirement.
  d of a long and tedious process,
   individuals emerged from a lengthy
 bilities, representing major currents
   typographic design. Modernism,
   ual design, typographic expressionism,
   nism, classicism, and experimental
   are each represented.

 ofiled designers enable readers to view a
 ma of American typographic design.
 rnist pioneers such as Paul Rand and
 dbury Thompson (who continue to make
 r presence known) take their place alongside
 t-modernist April Greiman, the rationalist
 ssimo Vignelli, and the eccentric eclectic
 ila Scher. Frank Armstrong has invented a
 thodology based upon the relationship
 tween music and typography, while Willi
 inz solves typographic problems based upon
 alogous relationships between architecture
  d typography.

 hile as much objectivity was built into the
 ction process as possible, the task of choosing
 representational group of designers will
 ndoubtedly fall victim to a degree of subjectivity.
Some readers may feel that a favorite designer
has been "skipped over." It is hoped that

regardless of personal preference, the profiled
designers will comprise an irresistible combination
of typographic approaches. Certainly, other
designers are equally deserving of recognition.

•

Part 2 presents a descriptive list of major
typographic resources. With the exception of
historical movements, these resources are confined
to the current century. Individuals, movements,
organizations, and periodicals are featured
in the broadest sense to reflect the interdisciplinary
nature of typographic design.

•

Throughout the designer profiles, important
influences are called out in **bold type.** These
items cue readers to the resources section where
additional information can be obtained on
each item. The resources section is organized
alphabetically for quick reference.

•

Rather than functioning as a definitive history
or assessment of American typography, this
book serves as a platform for further exploration
and as a source for visual inspiration. Unlike
the typical design annual, *American Typography
Today* is a substantive sourcebook of ideas
and factual information, filling an important
gap in current typographic literature.

A note about terminology

The terms "typographic designer" and "typographer" are often used synonymously. However,
fine distinctions exist between them. A "typographic designer" is someone who works with
type, arranging it in space for effective communication. A "typographer" is someone who also
works with type; but the term may also refer
to the operator of a typesetting machine, or the
director of a typesetting company. A "graphic
designer" identifies, examines, and solves
communication problems using a wide range of
tools, processes, and visual/verbal language
skills. While typography — making thoughts
visible — is a fundamental tool for the graphic
designer, images are another. Ultimately
these designations are not of great concern, for
what matters most is the attitude about typography that each practitioner brings to his work.

Twenty-Four American Typographic Designers

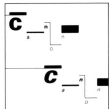

Frank Armstrong

1

Is design more closely related to art or to science? Frank Armstrong has excelled in both areas, proving that it is not a question of choosing between one or the other, but of synthesizing both into a feasible methodology.

During his early education, Armstrong studied mathematics and science, developing skills in structured problem solving. After graduating from UCLA, he was asked by Ted Wu to join his Los Angeles design firm. It was here that Armstrong began a fervent romance with typography. His first experience with letterforms was to burnish Helvetica press type to architectural signage. Although this process was archaic and tedious, it was also intimate and tactile, and it led him to observe the subtle beauty of letterform design and the intricate nature of interletter spacing. These early experiences provided Armstrong with skills of both logic and intuition.

Other influences have enriched Armstrong's thinking. His formal typographic education was supplemented by the writings of **Emil Ruder,** who introduced him to the visual characteristics of typography, and those of **Wassily Kandinsky,** who inspired him to experiment with the vi   nteraction of typographic el   ts within a composition. As a student at Yale University, Armstrong's association with **Alvin Eisenman, Paul Rand,** and **Bradbury Thompson** provided an historical perspective. Inge Druckery helped him to more effectively organize and evaluate visual compositions.

Joan Heller, a singer of contemporary classical music with extraordinary vocal capabilities, opened Armstrong's mind to the abstract and emotional potentials of typography. Creating beautiful abstract sounds with her voice through variations in pitch, dynamics, and texture, Heller simultaneously communicates the content and emotional qualities of the text. Armstrong discovered that there is a profound similarity in the communicative qualities of music and typographic design, for typography also has the potential to communicate the content and emotional qualities of a text through visual arrangement and thought-unit phrasing. This was a breakthrough from the more "rigidly

2

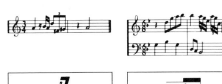

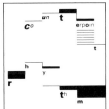

3

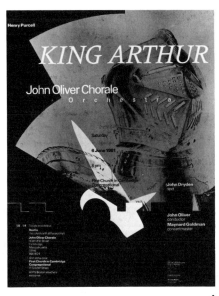

4

Frank Armstrong (born in 1949 in Evanston, Illinois) is President of Armstrong Design Consultants, specializing in annual reports, signage programs, identity and marketing programs, publication systems, and software for typographic formats. He received a BA degree in economics from UCLA in 1971 and an MFA degree in graphic design from Yale University in 1978. Awards of excellence include the American Institute of Graphic Arts, *Communication Arts*, 11th International Poster Biennale, and the Type Directors Club.

structured" design approach of his earlier architectural signage. Without abandoning his commitment to functional design, Armstrong put his energy into exploring the emotional qualities inherent in typographic form while "maintaining a concern for the abstract visual qualities of a composition and its function."

The eye flows through Armstrong's typographic scores of pulsating rhythms and dynamic spaces. "My unique vision of typographic design," says Armstrong, "is based upon a theoretical equivalence between visual and aural spatial fields. I believe that there is an analogous relationship between typography and music: the pulsating 'rhythm' of typographic elements and spaces as the eye moves across visual compositions, the various 'harmonies' created by texts set with different amounts of leading,

1   Illustrations for an unpublished article on typographic design.

2–4   Concert posters for the John Oliver Chorale.

5   Symbol used to identify a series of concerts.

Frank Armstrong

6

7

the visual 'dynamics' of various type weights. I evaluate my typographic compositions in terms of their musical characteristics."

This unique idea is demonstrated in Armstrong's book *Visual Forms and Sound* (Figs. 6,7). The text of this large-format, limited-edition book demonstrates the principles of typographic rhythm, melody, and harmony, directly linking the structural qualities of music to typography. The brassy sound of a trumpet, the mellow muses of a clarinet, the rich array of sounds vibrating from a piano are all translated as qualities into the visual field. At one point in the book Armstrong elegantly translates a piece of music by Arnold Schoenberg.

The potent qualities associated with Armstrong's integration of aural and visual fields are varied, and they invite a reader to a multisensory communication experience. As the eye sees, the mind "hears" the words in response to their visual treatment. Adjustments in size, weight, spacing, positioning, and color reveal vivid auditory landscapes that give the illusion of three dimensions. Every element is carefully orchestrated, yet never forced. The ITT Programming Poster is a masterful example of Armstrong's ability to communicate with expressive and emotional power (Fig. 8). Intricate relationships define the structure of the poster. Three-dimensional forms, representing parts of four letters, float independently in a black field. Words and phrases, descriptive of the poster's theme of productivity and quality, emerge from deep space, revealing a hierarchy of information.

Although the work of Armstrong is energetic and forceful, a viewer always senses compositional order and refinement. In *Visual Forms and Sound*, Armstrong clarifies his position on the subject of functional typography: "A primary consideration of visual communications is the development of an informational syntax: distinct groups of visual information within an ordered sequence."

harmony = vertical repetitions

increased duration = increased letterspacing

increased volume = vertical extension

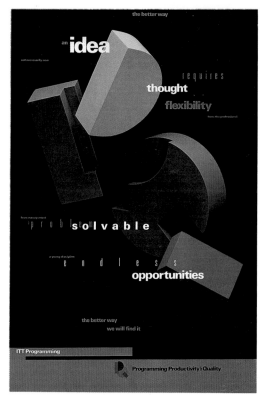

8

Armstrong has developed a precise methodology
for the solution of typographic problems:

Define the problem and objectives.

Define the parameters that influence the effectiveness of the solution.

Organize the information into functional groups.

Draw a schematic diagram indicating the
relationships between groups.

Assign a relative hierarchical value to each group.

Draw a schematic plan of the composition
including a visual tracking diagram.

Design a precise structural grid for the composition.

Assign typographical values to each functional group.

Create a prototype.

Evaluate the effectiveness of the solution relative
to the initial parameters.

Evaluate the visual aspects of the composition.

9

Armstrong is currently employing this methodology in the development of computer-
assisted, page-composition procedures. His use
of sound/space equivalencies to establish a
practical design methodology has revealed an
entire range of new possibilities in the field
of typographic communication.

6,7   Pages from a limited-edition book
       entitled *Visual Forms + Sound.*

8,9   Posters for ITT Programming.

Wilburn O. Bonnell III

Bill Bonnell's most valuable design resource is his remarkable visual memory; he is able to recall details of images and objects long after they have faded from sight. This, combined with an interest in all aspects of the designed environment—from buildings to cars—has resulted in a fluent command of form and a panoramic approach to design.

He received his education in industrial design at the University of Illinois. Its curriculum provided him with a knowledge of processes and materials, as well as unique experiences in problem solving. He vividly remembers, for example, a challenging and enlightening class he took from the biochemist Heinz von Foerster. Von Foerster motivated the students of this class—numbering over a hundred from various fields—to conceive, write, design, and produce a publication called *The Whole University Catalog*.

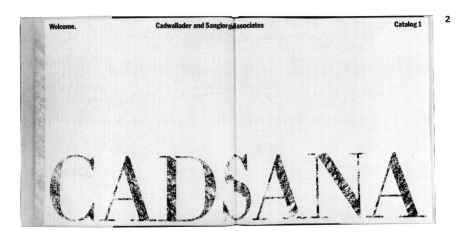

Welcome. Cadwallader and Sangiorgi Associates Catalog 1

1–3 Cover and interior spreads from a catalog for Cadsana, manufacturers of office systems and furniture.

4 Logotype for RyderTypes.

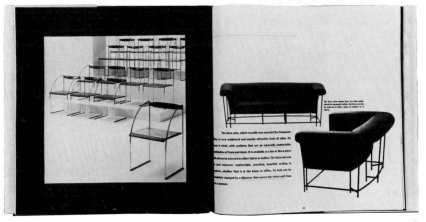

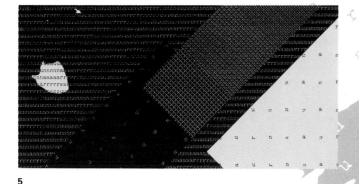

Wilburn O. Bonnell III (born in 1948
in Shelbyville, Illinois) is President of
Bonnell Design Associates, Inc., New
York. He studied industrial design at
the University of Illinois and in 1970
was named the Industrial Design
Society of America's Student of the
Year. He joined Container Corporation
of America in 1971, becoming Manager of Design in 1974. He has received many national and international awards, has served on the
board of the American Institute of
Graphic Arts, and is a member of
the Alliance Graphique Internationale.

The interactive process of this diverse group
brought Bonnell to the important understanding
that design resources can and should come
from anywhere.

As an industrial design student, Bonnell came
to realize how crucial letterforms are to the
overall appearance of products. One summer
while working for Robert Vogele in Chicago, he
was subjected to rigorous typographic discipline
for the first time. Vogele had a splendid
collection of design periodicals that he wanted
to organize and display within the office.
Bonnell was asked to create dividers for the
magazines by positioning black Helvetica press
type as labels onto white Masonite panels.
For an entire week Bonnell shifted letters back
and forth and up and down until the panels
were specimens of complete harmony and until
Vogele nodded his head in approval.

Bonnell entered the design profession able to
work as both an industrial and graphic designer.
He placed no artificial barriers between the
processes of these two areas of design activity.
With the extremely sophisticated sense of form
he had developed by this time, it is not
surprising that he became a disciple of an

5   Postcard for Sunar.

6   Poster encouraging people to vote.

Wilburn O. Bonnell III

7

8

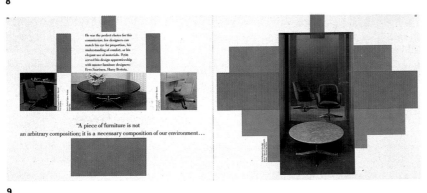

9

objective approach to visual communication that had migrated into America's corporate environment during the 1950s and 1960s, reaching its peak during the early 1970s.

This approach, which is rooted in Modernism and is directly linked to the Swiss movement, has been called the **International Typographic Style.** Bonnell was tremendously influenced by a number of sources that addressed this rational approach, including the ***Ulm Journals,*** a publication of the Ulm School of Design in Germany; ***New Graphic Design,*** a Swiss magazine; and the writings of **Josef Muller-Brockmann** and **Karl Gerstner.**

After joining **Container Corporation of America** in 1970, Bonnell quickly became one of America's leading practitioners of objective visual design. His work during this period is characterized by the use of seemingly contextureless geometric form, primary color, and sans serif type cleanly organized within neutral typographic grids. Bonnell's design solutions, which loyally serve their communication purpose, are aesthetically appealing due to formal clarity and precision, and due to Bonnell's exquisite use of paper and printing processes. Affinity towards materials is an extension of his industrial design background.

Many American designers became disillusioned with the objective approach to design towards the end of the 1970s, and Bonnell was among them. This approach seemed no longer relevant to the new post-industrial (post-modern) society. World conditions had changed drastically since the end of World War II: dwindling resources and advancements in technology were partly responsible for a shift in societal attitudes. Many designers responded with a more humanistic approach to visual problem solving. "I originally believed in objectivity and the principles of Objective Visual Design," says Bonnell. "Maturity brought me to an attitude of informed subjectivity— the designer's conscious point-of-view considered within broad social and human concerns."

7–9 Interior spreads from a 1982 catalog for Sunar, a manufacturer of office systems and furniture.

This change in direction became noticeable when he opened his New York design office. Many of his clients over the years have been those whose subject matter enable a more expressive posture. His lavish catalog designs for Sunar office systems, for example, express the qualities associated with the work of various furniture designers. The pages of these publications are playgrounds of form whose sensuous variety is established through high-quality photography, typographical contrasts, rich color, and interplays of contrasting symmetries. Each turn of a page offers a new surprise, and yet order is maintained through recurring visual themes (Figs. 7–11).

In a furniture catalog for Cadsana, Bonnell achieves an unequaled level of elegance, quality, and expression. Loosely scrawled textures found on the dust jacket, end sheets, title pages, and division pages, suggest the tactile quality of furniture coverings and establish a counterpoint to the geometrical lines of the typography and photographs. Typographic rules highlight product descriptions within the highly legible text, reference the formal qualities of the photographs, and serve as compositional anchors (Figs. 1–3). The iconic messages established by Bonnell's ingenious manipulation of form and material clearly reveal the quality and standards of this furniture manufacturer.

Those who experience Bonnell's visual communication feel as though they are participants in the communication rather than just receivers of messages. This interactive quality supports his view that "Graphic communication should as much as possible mimic human verbal interaction types such as dialogue, conversation, poetry, and drama. Graphic communication is always a substitute or an amplification of what would ideally be communicated in a spoken conversation between two people."

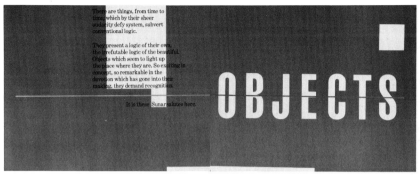

10

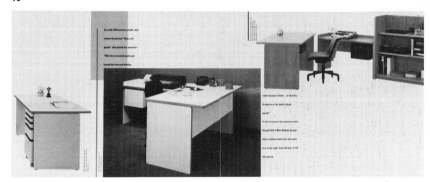

11

10,11   Interior spreads from a 1983 catalog for Sunar, a manufacturer of office systems and furniture.

12   Calendar for Container Corporation of America.

12

Ronn Campisi

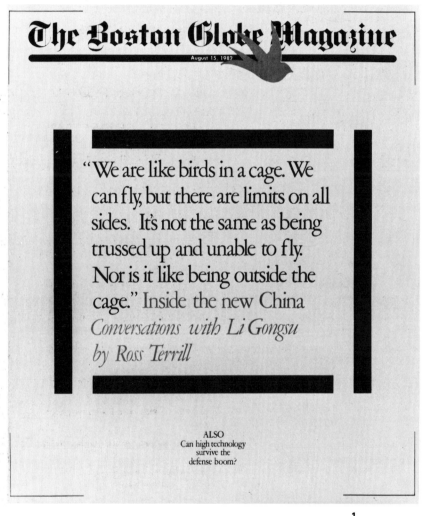

Ronn Campisi became aware of "design" as something that people do when he was about seven years old, and what he wanted to design at this early age was cars! "When I was about nine," Campisi remembers, "I was seriously influenced by *Mad Magazine*, and my sensibilities shifted from cars to magazines, and I decided at that point I wanted to design them. I made my own pretend magazines with a typewriter, cut-out pictures, and press type. I became interested in playing with the appearance and shapes of words using different letterforms. At nine years old I had no idea what I was doing, other than having fun. However, everything I do with type and design to this day is an extension of that experience . . . playing with shapes, forms, words to create pictures of ideas."

The make-believe magazines that Campisi so feverishly assembled as a child evolved over the years into a major American publication of distinction. As former art director of *The Boston Globe Magazine*, Campisi redesigned the magazine's format, producing some of the most memorable magazine covers and interior spreads of the eighties. This accomplishment is all the more significant when one remembers that this is a weekly magazine, and each week Campisi and his staff produced a new edition, each one as outstanding as the last. The magazine's short turnaround time forced him to work quickly—a limitation that can stifle the most capable of designers, but that gave Campisi the opportunity to bring freshness and spontaneity to the publication.

Magazine design in America tends to be extremely eclectic, and "new ideas" are volleyed back and forth as soon as periodicals hit the newsstand. Imitation is quietly accepted, but no one admits to it—every designer wants to believe that everyone else is borrowing from him. During the early eighties, handfuls of publications such as *The Boston Globe Magazine*, *Esquire*, and *The New York Times Magazine*, shared common stylistic traits. Of course, each of these magazines had its own merits, but Campisi breathed a rare intensity and vigor into his publication.

The Boston Globe Magazine

From a new book by Sissela Bok

MILITARY SECRECY

Scientists developing the atomic bomb
believed they could make war so evil it
would be rejected forever. Insulated
by tight security from outside opinion,
they heard no dissenting views.

2

The Boston Globe Magazine

REPORTING ON THE THIRD REICH

*How the press
misjudged the menace
of Hitler*

3

"Style" is one of those ambiguous terms that is
difficult to pin down. Campisi firmly believes
that individualism has a lot to do with the
making of design: "There are certain design
devices and ways of doing things that add
up to a defined 'style.' Some sense of this 'style'
is related to the time frame in which the
work was created. What I designed in the
seventies looks different from what I design in
the eighties. Other parts of it come from
within; the way in which a designer processes
information and thinks about the world."

Words are at the center of publication design—
prepackaged words, which must be converted
into tangible typographic form that is imaginative,
readable, and true to the author's intent. Says
Campisi: "Everything that is printed on a page,
or a screen, gives a reader a visual clue about
the kind of message that is being conveyed. By
using photographs, symbols, art and type, a
picture is created. Before one word is even read,
a reader responds instantly to that picture and
establishes an opinion about it." Campisi
treats typography as a visual code that intensifies

Ronn Campisi (born in 1947 in Boston,

Massachusetts) is President of Ronn

Campisi Design. He was educated

at the Art Institute of Boston. As

the former design director of *The

Boston Globe,* he received over 300

awards for his work. In 1983 he was

part of a team that won a Pulitzer

Prize for a special magazine section

entitled "War and Peace in the Nu-

clear Age." His work has appeared in

Graphis Annual as well as *Graphis*

magazine, the Type Directors Club

Annual, *Print,* and *Communication

Arts.* He lectures and judges design

competitions frequently.

1–3 Covers from the *Boston
Globe Magazine.*

Ronn Campisi

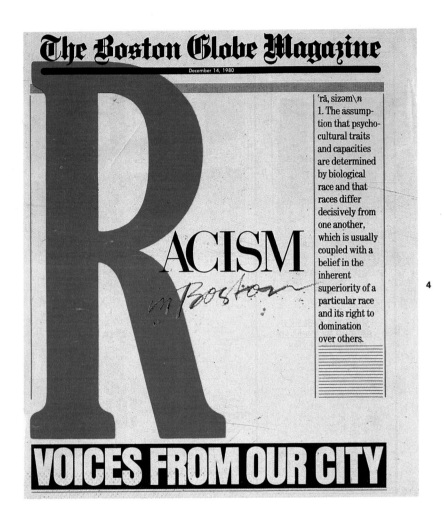

'rā, sizəm\ n
1. The assumption that psycho-cultural traits and capacities are determined by biological race and that races differ decisively from one another, which is usually coupled with a belief in the inherent superiority of a particular race and its right to domination over others.

4

5

4–6   Covers from the *Boston Globe Magazine.* Photographer for "Zimbabwe's Winds of Change": Stan Grosveld.

7   Interior spread from the *Boston Globe Magazine.* Illustration: Gene Greif.

verbal meaning. Because the code must be accurate for a message to be effective, every decision the designer makes, including the choice of typeface, is critical; for letterforms have the innate ability to express meaning in and of themselves.

Campisi's mastery of visible words can be largely attributed to his passion for magazine design. But ardor alone does not always bring results—one must look to the past for proper context. The legacy of publication design left by such preeminent designers as **M. F. Agha,** who in 1929 signaled the advent of the modern magazine with his design of *Vanity Fair*; and others such as **Alexey Brodovitch, Paul Rand,** and **Otto Storch** have most certainly contributed to the shaping of an entire generation of designers. Their influence has led designers to understand the relationship between typographic form and editorial content.

Campisi is highly sensitive to the subtle visual qualities of type; he puts into action a conviction held by **Aaron Burns:** "Modern typography, with its emphasis on simplicity and brevity, does not consider any good typeface to be dated. On the contrary, . . . a simple letter a hundred or more years old may combine well with a most recent face, as does serif and sans serif, script and gothic. In short, there should be no rule except to make typography pleasing to the eye."

Campisi's view of the world is reflected in his cover designs, which he uses as an expressive medium to convert ordinary words into powerful typographic images. His covers challenge readers, tease them into the magazine, and function as a record of our time. To look at one of Campisi's covers is to be held captive by the power of visible words. One particularly gripping example addresses the problem of racism in Boston (Fig. 4). The word *racism* functions as a typographic sign composed of two contrasting typefaces. A Cheltenham *R* demonstrates the racial issues of inequality, superiority, and domination by its size, color, and style. The remaining letters of the word are set in the timid, though elegant, Bauer Bodoni. This cover typifies Campisi's crisp, bold, and highly refined typographic approach.

Campisi's philosophy of design is very simple; he feels that there are no secret formulas for creating good work. "A designer needs luck, good people to work with, and good ideas that are simple and direct. A designer needs support from clients, the freedom to think and express ideas, and the freedom to make mistakes."

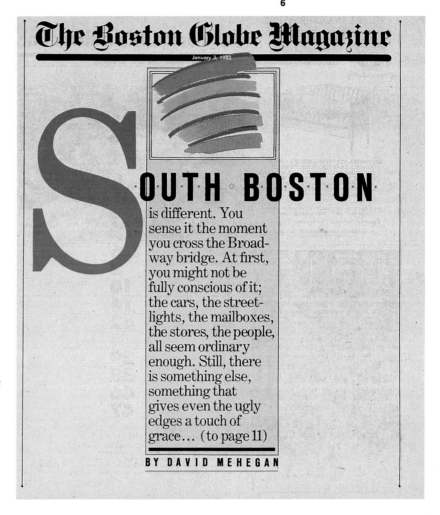

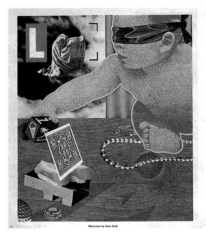

Jacqueline S. Casey

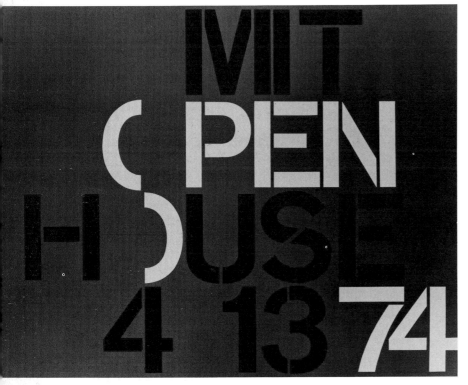

1

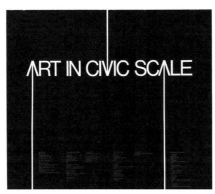

2

When Jacqueline Casey entered the Office of Design at MIT for on-the-job training as a graphic designer, it was not long before she developed a personal and highly rational typographic style that became the trademark of print communication for the university. It is a simple and restrained style, rich in meaning and capable of tremendous variety. Casey's methodical mind distills complex and abstract information into potent and memorable signs. She believes that the strength of typographic design lies in the objective presentation of information based on the elemental principles of visual form.

Upon her arrival at MIT, Casey was introduced to **Muriel Cooper**—her first teacher/art director and most significant influence. From Cooper she learned about the design process and about gathering information to solve visual problems. Therese Moll, who also worked at MIT for a short time, was a Swiss designer whose gift to Casey was a working knowledge of the grid and of **Swiss typography.** Casey's interest in typographic clarity was fueled by the work and writings of **Josef Muller-Brockmann, Armin Hofmann,** and Kurt Wirth.

In keeping with the tenets of the Swiss approach, Casey equates beauty with function. Needless ornament has no place in her work. Rather, her work possesses a simplicity and subtle beauty not easily forgotten. Form and color—integral parts of a message—are harmoniously woven into a total design. Usually, a typographic image surrounded by open space forms the nucleus of a message, and assumes a dominant position in the visual hierarchy through size, placement, and color. Straightforward typography, usually Helvetica or a similar sans serif typeface, is used to present descriptive information. A tight grid controls the structure of the composition.

"The image is the message" is a phrase transformed into action by Casey as she masterfully combines the verbal and visual attributes of typography into images reflecting the essence of a message. Under Casey's spell, ordinary words are transformed into images that challenge the mind

1   Poster for an MIT open house.

2   Poster for a conference.

3

4

Jacqueline S. Casey (born in 1927 in
Quincy, Massachusetts) has been a
graphic designer at MIT since 1955.
She received a certificate in Fashion
Design and Illustration and a BFA
degree from the Massachusetts College of Art. Her work has been exhibited throughout the world and is
in the permanent collection of several museums, including the Museum
of Modern Art, Cooper-Hewitt Museum, and the Library of Congress.
She is a member of the Alliance
Graphique Internationale and her
work has been featured in numerous
books and periodicals. In 1982, MIT,
under the direction of Casey, was
awarded the Design Leadership
Award by the American Institute of
Graphic Arts.

and require the viewer to participate. Her
designs invite the audience not only to see, but
also to understand. For example, a poster
announcing an exhibition that documents artists'
and architects' proposals for a public transportation project combines curved and straight
lines to form the letters of the title *Arts on the
Line* (Fig. 5). This image playfully reinforces
the content of the message.

By researching a given problem thoroughly,
Casey makes unusual connections by contrasting
two or more opposing signs. This principle
can be compared to spoken language where
meaning is derived from the contrast and com-
parison of words within a sentence: when
words are shuffled, meaning changes. Casey
uses a similar approach in her designs by
combining dissimilar typographic forms into an
ordered arrangement, thereby establishing
specific meaning. A compelling poster, for
example, illustrates this approach by ingeniously

3   Poster for an MIT pollution project.

4   Poster for a sculpture exhibition.

Art for Public Transit Spaces

An Exhibition Documenting Artists'
Proposals and Architects' Designs for the
MBTA Red Line Northwest Extension:
Harvard Square Station
Porter Square Station
Davis Square Station
Alewife Station

Hayden Gallery and Hayden Corridor Gallery
Massachusetts Institute of Technology
Hayden Library Memorial Building
160 Memorial Drive
Cambridge, Massachusetts 02139

Public Reception: February 8, 6 to 8 pm
Artists and Architects Will Attend

February 9 through March 16, 1980
Gallery Hours 10 to 4 Daily
Wednesday Evening 6 to 9
Telephone:
Gallery 253-4680, Office 253-4400

Illustrated Catalogue and Videotaped Critique
"Conversations on Public Art" Available

Organized by the MIT Committee on the
Visual Arts in Collaboration with
The Cambridge Arts Council. Arts on the Line
is a Pilot Project of the United States
Department of Transportation
through the Urban Mass Transportation
Administration and the Massachusetts Bay
Transportation Authority

Jacqueline S. Casey

ARTS ON THE LINE

5   Poster for an exhibition of art for
    public transit spaces in Boston.

6   Peace poster.

6

making a plea for world peace. It fuses alter-
nating red and white letters into two words
that signify the peaceful coexistence of Russia
and the United States (Fig. 6). The context
of this typographic unit is established by
the placement of the planet earth, appearing
as a shadow, in the upper-right portion of
the space.

Design for Casey is a personal and private affair.
She objects to premature comments from
others while in the thick of problem solving.
The process that she follows to get to a solution
is as simple and direct as the work itself.
Research, a fundamental step in the process,
includes collecting information from libraries,
museums, laboratories, and other pertinent
sources. Having collected diverse materials on
the subject, she begins to make connections by
comparing ideas, sketching them, discarding
them, and sketching again. Color and a variety
of materials are tools in this process. Casey's
methods have not changed significantly since the
early years at MIT: "In those days I had to
trace letterforms from cards supplied by type
houses. This constant tracing produced a
knowledge of typefaces and a sense of how
letters interact with each other and with the
spaces around them. Tracing and drawing

Six Artists

Hardu Keck
David Kibbey
Katherine Porter
Robert Rohm
Anthony Thompson
Dan Wills

Hayden Gallery
Massachusetts Institute
of Technology
May 13 – September 6, 1970
Opening May 12, 8-10 pm
Artists will be present

Sponsored by the
MIT Committee on the
Visual Arts

letterforms is an aesthetic experience for me."
Casey has experimented with other tools such as
the typewriter and the IBM Composer. Press
type was also used as a design tool because
of the diversity of letterforms and the availability
of new typefaces, which gave her more latitude
for typographic experimentation and play.

It is obvious from this description of her
design process that Casey relies heavily upon
traditional tools and materials in her typographic
work. She approaches the subject of computer
technology with reserved optimism: "I am
mainly concerned with the quality and diversity
of the typographic and graphic images produced
by computers. I am sure that the situation
will continue to improve as more creative
designers get involved with technology."

Concern with quality and clear transmission of
visual information is at the center of Casey's
design philosophy: "Quite simply, my objective
is to design a product with an accurate visual
and verbal message that can be understood
by the audience." Memorable forms become a
source of visual satisfaction, challenging the
viewer's mind: "I measure my success as a
designer when the work is displayed on and off
campus when the event is a memory."

8

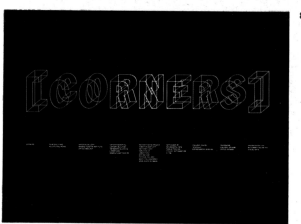

7   **Poster for an exhibition featuring
     the work of six British artists.**

8   **Poster for an exhibition of
     painterly sculpture.**

David Colley

1

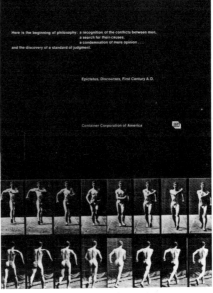

The American Music Group
Neely Bruce, Director

Works by Billings, Denson, Fillmore,
Heinrich, Lancaster, Mason, Pease,
Root, Warden, White, Work, and other
American composers.

A performance at the Depot
223 North Broadway, Urbana
November 1, 2, 3, 4, 1973 8:00 pm

Tickets 1.50 at Record Service
704 South Sixth Street Champaign
and at the Depot on performance nights

Design fads have no place in David Colley's life. He is a functionalist with a restless and searching intelligence who approaches typographic design as a process of structured thought. A blend of experiences—beginning in Kentucky where he received informal training from his grandmother in piano playing and baking, and ending in New York at Columbia University where he studied art history—shaped his mind, solidified his interests, and formed his sensitive nature.

Colley considers himself lucky, for he launched his study of typography in a composing room full of metal type, methodically placing type into a composing stick and printing it in the bed of a proof press. Through this process he learned about the formal beauty of individual letters and the tactile quality of metal type impressions. Perhaps more importantly, he learned about the physical limitations of this early technology and about the structural character of metal type. This, more than anything else, provided him with a sound basis for designing with type in light of current technologies— even type that is digitally produced on photographic paper. For Colley, the greatest reward in working with typography is "understanding structure and limitations and making attempts to invent, despite those structures and limitations."

2

1 Poster for a concert featuring the
   work of American composers.

2 Advertisement for Container
   Corporation of America.

Design history—particularly the formative experiments of the **Bauhaus,** and what Colley calls "the codification of the 'modern' typographic vocabulary by German and Swiss schools"—validated his personal commitment to structure and objectivity in design. The work of **Josef Muller-Brockmann** enhanced Colley's understanding of the beauty and clarity of objective visual communication, and opened his mind to the many possibilities associated with rational design.

In America, the work of **Massimo Vignelli** demonstrated to him how objectivity in design could be rich, inventive, and joyful. In 1975, while a designer at the Office of Design Services at MIT, the presence of German-educated **Dietmar Winkler** inspired Colley to a new level of typographic discipline and contributed to that office's unsurpassed level of quality in design.

Since his early days at the piano, music has been important to Colley's development. He is now an accomplished pianist who finds that music and typography are similarly structured, each having the potential to communicate structure and its expansion and extension. Many great composers have captured Colley's imagination, but he is most fascinated by the genius

3

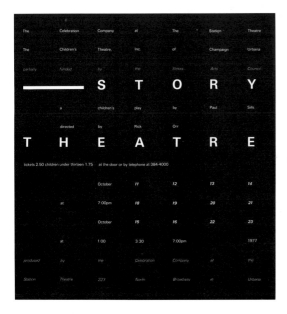

4

David Colley (born in 1940 in Mayfield, Kentucky) is a freelance design consultant and Professor of Design at the University of Illinois. He received an MA degree in art history from Columbia University in 1964 and an MFA degree in graphic design from the University of Illinois in 1969. His work has been featured in numerous design periodicals and books, has been exhibited widely, and is part of several permanent collections, including the Museum of Modern Art, Smithsonian Institution, Library of Congress, Staatliches Museum fur Angewande Kunst, Munich, and the Georges Pomidou Center, Paris.

3   Poster for the Joffery Ballet.

4   Poster for *Story Theatre.*

David Colley

School of Music
Krannert Center for the Performing Arts
University of Illinois at Urbana-Champaign

a program to commemorate the hundredth birthday of Alban Berg

B E R G

Saturday 9 February 1985
Foellinger Great Hall 8:00 pm

Vier Lieder, Op. 2 (1909-1910)
Barbara Dalheim, *soprano*
Eric Dalheim, *piano*

Adagio (1935)
second movement from the *Chamber Concerto*
Catherine Tait, *violin*
Howard Klug, *clarinet*
Eric Dalheim, *piano*

Vier Stücke, Op. 5 (1913)
Howard Klug, *clarinet*
David Liptak, *piano*

5   Poster for the musical production,
   Sweeney Todd.

6   Poster for a program commemo-
   rating the hundreth birthday of
   Alban Berg.

7   Announcement for an open house
   at the School of Art and Design,
   University of Illinois.

8   Poster for the play, *Vanities.*

of one: "Perhaps my greatest teacher has been W. A. Mozart—especially the piano sonatas where structure is so beautifully stated and then so gloriously released."

Early in his career, Colley's work was rigid, tight, and bound to a specific agenda. Over the years, he has become more malleable and evolutionary, finding great pleasure in seeing his work extend beyond old, self-imposed boundaries into new possibilities. For example, he is no longer a slave to the standard typographic grid; he allows structure to evolve out of the unique nature of the content, resulting in a more dynamic and expressive distribution of typographic forms.

Colley possesses the eye of a detached and objective observer, maintaining a sense of purpose and direction about his work. This same sense is used to reveal the essence of messages by squeezing meaning out of typographic signs. A poster designed to announce a concert of American music, for example, introduces a slightly warped, floating title recalling gentle, rhythmic sounds, or possibly a waving flag (Fig. 1). Appropriate red, white, and blue colors enhance signification. Visual communication, for Colley, is akin to verbal communication; each is based upon specific structural laws. As a means to better understand the nature of visual language, he refers to models found in structural linguistics and anthropology; he is a student of **Claude Levi-Strauss, Ferdinand de Saussure,** and **Roland Barthes.**

Colley is at home with the poster, having produced hundreds of them over the years. He uses this medium to explore the nature of visual language, and the diverse ways in which typographic messages can be generated. A poster for the play *Vanities* (Fig. 8), features large type printed at an oblique angle in a complete spectrum of gradated colors, emerging from a grey background to suggest the temperament associated with the human trait vanity. In another example, type dramatically slices through a blood-red field, signifying the knife of Sweeney Todd (Fig. 5). Both of these posters demonstrate Colley's distinctive use of

visual language, and are composed of forms that remodel ordinary words into metaphors of intensified meaning.

To the degree that ambiguity occurs in his work, it serves to strengthen the connotative and poetic nature of the message, and to challenge the viewer. He does not indulge his audience, and often expects them to meet him at the midpoint of message transmission. The subtle sophistication of Colley's work raises awareness and demands viewer attention.

Colley's typographic solutions stretch the boundaries of everyday language. They come from within—his mind being his most valued resource: "The discovery of the structure of thinking, its exploitation, and finally its expansion, is an essential part of design practice."

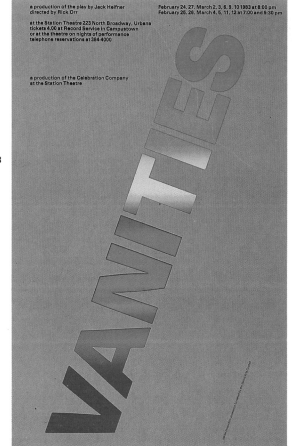

8

Louis Dorfsman

When most people think of CBS, they think of network news and television entertainment. Designers, however, think of Lou Dorfsman. He has been with CBS for over forty years, shaping the image of this company with intelligence, sophistication, and humor. And while he may be recognized primarily as an "ad-man," this label falls far short of describing the encompassing activities of Dorfsman. "Master-planner" is a more appropriate term, for in leading the destiny of one of the largest communication corporations in the world, he has been involved with all aspects of the business—research, marketing and sales, programming, advertising and exhibition design, filmmaking and architectural graphics.

Worth Repeating

The Columbia Broadcasting System turned in a superb journalistic beat last night, running away with the major honors in reporting President Johnson's election victory. In clarity of presentation the network led all the way... In a medium where time is of the essence the performance of CBS was of landslide proportions. The difference...lay in the CBS sampling process called Vote Profile Analysis...the CBS staff called the outcome in state after state before its rivals. JACK GOULD, The New York Times (11/4)

1

1 Full-page newspaper advertisement for CBS News.

2,3 First two pages and title spread from a book on the first moon-landing as reported.

2

3

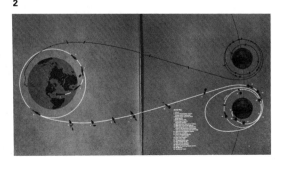

10:56:20PM 72069

It all began when he was a student at Cooper Union. The classes that he took were certainly important to his development, but perhaps even more important were the cultural experiences outside of school and the friendships he formed during this period. **Herb Lubalin** was a classmate, and the two of them maintained a strong bond, both professionally and socially for nearly forty years. While at Cooper Union he worked part time painting signs until he found a job with Display Guild, a firm that was producing exhibits for the 1939 World's Fair. This was a formative experience for Dorfsman, for it was here that he met his mentor Bob McGuire, an industrial designer who taught him about materials, three-dimensional structures, and other sundry topics that broadened his view of the world.

In 1946, Dorfsman was hired by **William Golden,** the Creative Director of CBS, as an assistant. In the years that followed, he studied Golden's ingenious advertising methods, absorbing as many of them into his own vocabulary as he possibly could. In 1951, after CBS management divided the company into two separate divisions—radio and television— Dorfsman was asked to become art director of the Radio Network. In this position he faced the formidable challenge of keeping radio alive in a television-oriented society. In late 1959, with the sudden death of Golden, Dorfsman became Creative Director for the CBS Television Network, and subsequently was promoted to Senior Vice President and Creative Director of the CBS Broadcast Group.

Dorfsman is as comfortable with words as he is with pictures, and before he ever puts pencil to paper he is able to articulate ideas thoroughly. He believes that good ideas come from the methodical study of design problems, and indeed, he looks at every angle. "For him," writes Dick Hess and Marion Muller in *Dorfsman & CBS,* "the project starts with studying the client's problems, understanding his business, figuring out what has to be said and how best to say it. Most often the words are in his head before the picture—a strange sequence of

4

Louis Dorfsman (born in 1918 in New York City) is Vice President and Creative Director of Advertising and Design, CBS Inc. He graduated from the Cooper Union School of Art and Architecture with a BFA. Over the years he has received numerous national and international awards for his work, including Cooper Union's highest alumni award, the Augustus St. Gaudens medal. In 1978 he was elected to the Art Directors Club Hall of Fame and received the prestigious AIGA Gold Medal.

4 "Gastrotypographicalassemblage." (Detail)

5 Exterior signage for the CBS headquarters building, featuring the typeface, CBS Didot.

Louis Dorfsman

6

7

events for an art director! All design decisions about layout, typography, illustration, etc., follow from the idea."

With Dorfsman's ability to express himself in words, it is understandable that typography often becomes the subject matter of his designs. His words are found in their visual form on hundreds of advertisements and other graphic materials. One well-known example was designed to inform the public that CBS had the three best comedy programs. Cold statistics are transformed into warm laughter with "ha ha ha" representing a bar chart that compares the three major networks (Fig. 8). When Dorfsman uses type as subject matter, it is chosen for its expressive characteristics; when he uses it as text, his overriding concern is legibility.

Because solutions grow from problems, Dorfsman does not operate within a specific visual style. What is consistent, however, is the craftsmanship and quality that guides each project through to completion. And whether he is working on a project so basic as a single-column newspaper ad, or so complex as a corporate identity program, he approaches each with the precision of an engineer. No typographic detail is too small to be considered unimportant.

For example, in 1964 Dorfsman was asked to coordinate and design all of the interior and exterior graphics of the new corporate headquarters building in New York. His charge was to create a graphics program that would enhance the building (designed by Eero Saarinen) and express the corporate personality. He began by designing the corporate typeface, a version of the elegant seventeenth-century typeface, Didot. Named CBS Didot, this face provided a counterpoint to the massive quality of the building (Fig. 5). In addition, a companion sans serif typeface called CBS Sans was designed by **Freeman Craw** for secondary use. These faces were applied to everything typographic: clocks, room numbers, exit signs, letters

6 **Full-page newspaper advertisement for the CBS program, *The Rocket's Red Glare.***

7 **Advertisement for CBS. The copy celebrates the opening of the Lincoln Center's Philharmonic Hall.**

8

over the entrance doors, and even cafeteria dispensing machines. All corporate printed materials were also updated to harmonize with the building.

Within this unity of Dorfsman's corporate image is a magical diversity. His "Gastro-typographicalassemblage" is one example (Fig. 4). Collaborating with Lubalin and staff, he created this three-dimensional, thirty-eight foot mural for the cafeteria in the CBS headquarters building. The mural is a typographical collage of cutout words comprising 250 typefaces and 85 objects, all related to food. This sense of monumentality characterizes Dorfsman's attitudes about the untapped possibilities of design—attitudes that he brings to every project.

A sense of classicism, a concern for quality, and a need to clearly identify and solve problems are the qualities Dorfsman has exhibited during his years at CBS. These qualities have been vividly projected into America's culture, distinguishing him as one of the most influential designers of the century.

10

11

8   Advertisement for the CBS Television Network.

9–11   Full-page newspaper advertisements for CBS News.

Louise Fili

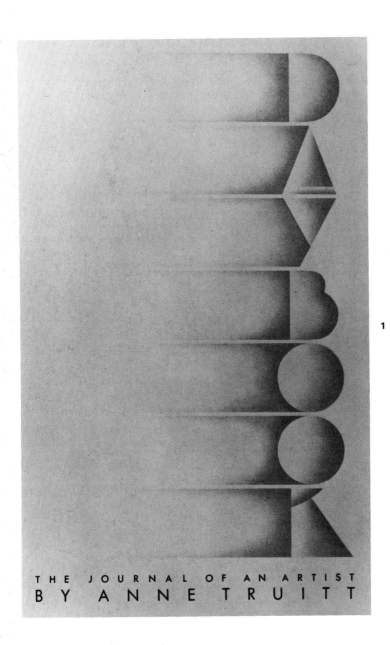

1 Book jacket for *Daybook*.

As early as age four, Louise Fili carved letterforms into the wall above her bed. This activity— merely childhood amusement at the time—now, after many years, symbolizes a lasting fascination with letterforms. Fili's uninhibited doodlings of childhood have been transformed into book typography of beauty and distinction.

Fili wanted to attend art school in New York, but her parents had other ideas. They thought it more proper for their daughter to get a good education at a sound liberal arts institution. So off she went to Skidmore College in Saratoga Springs, New York. The college had few offerings in graphic design; nonetheless, Fili knew that this was what she wanted to do. She spent a lot of time in the college press room working with metal type—an experience that proved extremely valuable, for it solidified her love of typography and she was able to assemble a portfolio of graphic work.

Determined to find a job, Fili moved to New York after graduation. She was willing to do almost anything to prepare herself as a designer and to make up for lost time. One of her first jobs was with B. Martin Pedersen's design office, where she worked for an intensive nine months. A period of freelance design followed, and for the first time Fili became involved with books and publishing. Random House and Knopf hired her to work on special projects. Perhaps the most pivotal move in her early career came when she took a job with **Herb Lubalin** Associates. Here she had the opportunity of working with Harris Lewine, an inspired art director of books and book jackets who influenced her greatly. Fili's passion for this genre grew steadily, until eventually she was working on book jackets almost exclusively. In 1978 she joined Pantheon Books.

2

Louise Fili (born in 1951 in Livingston, New Jersey) is an art director at Pantheon Books. In 1973, she received a BS degree in studio art from Skidmore College. As a designer specializing in book jackets, she has received much attention for her work, including Gold and Silver Medals from the New York Art Directors Club, and a Silver Medal from the Society of Illustrators. Major articles discussing her work have appeared in *Communication Arts*, *How*, *Art Direction*, and *Metropolis* magazines.

3

2   Book cover for *The WPA Guide to New York City.*

3   Book jacket for *The War.*

Louise Fili

4

Fili is primarily a designer of book jackets, but will occasionally take on entire books when budgets are high enough to make this long and arduous task worthwhile. With each project, she attempts to extend the boundaries of the genre by continually looking for new ways of combining type, ornament, illustration, and photography. With much of her inspiration coming from European designers of the thirties and forties, it is possible to discover several influences beneath the surface of her designs: the simplified, minimalist spaces of **Lucien Bernhard;** the Cubist tendencies of **A. M. Cassandre;** and the emotional, geometric forms of **Jean Carlu,** to name a few.

These influences, however, never overshadow Fili's personal vision and unique approach to typography: "I often create situations in typography that defy standard type. When I design a book jacket, I usually do tissue after tissue, where the type goes from an amorphous blob to a tightly focused form—in most cases, a typeface which does not in fact exist, which I will have hand lettered. I've come to believe that every jacket I design has one, and only one typeface that is just right—rarely one found in a type book." Fili's letterforms often defy traditional proportions; and typographic attributes such as stress, slant, weight, and width are altered to achieve unusual effects.

The oddities resulting from Fili's imaginative alterations bring charm and distinction to her jacket designs, and most certainly evoke viewer response. Sometimes the letterforms are as unexpected as some wood type specimens of the nineteenth century—cartoon-like, but more refined. Letterforms on a jacket for *When Things of the Spirit Come First,* emerge from the interplay of manufactured light and shadow (Fig. 7). These letters are mysteriously ethereal, having something of the quality of a Cassandre poster, with dissected, split, and fading planes shimmering on the surface of the paper. When Fili combines different letterforms into single compositions, she does not get caught up in "safe" juxtapositions; rather, she takes chances,

5   6

and her unexpected combinations seem to work. Letterforms having little in common are integrated with extreme care. While Fili's typography can be both outspoken and subdued, it is never inhibited.

"Filiisms" abound. Widely spaced letters, often textured, move airily across a page and defy established "rules" for book jacket design. And she has introduced other controversial ideas: small type, overlapping type, and borderline illegible type. She models letters from soft, pastel colors that are still taboo to some book publishers. The effect of these innovations is that her book jackets are more distinctive than most in crowded bookstores. A jacket for *The Lover* is striking for similar non-traditional reasons (Fig. 6). It combines a soft, vignette photograph with letters that similarly fade off at the edges. The geometrically precise typography frames and accentuates the haunting female portrait. This cover does not scream— it beckons.

Book jackets are typically regarded as ephemeral. Historically, when such short-lived objects move into the realm of art (as has happened with the poster), it is because of the infusion of profound personal expression. Fili's innovative, typographical jackets can certainly be classified as art.

7

Thomas H. Geismar

In the late 1950s, a group of young American designers with foresight and energy dissolved the superficial barriers separating diverse areas of design (advertising design, type design, book design, exhibition design, etc.). Instead, they approached the profession broadly, as "synthesizers" and "problem solvers," able to tackle a wide range of issues. Thomas Geismar was among those influential pioneers of a new, universal approach to design.

It is not surprising then, that he does not think of himself as a "typographic designer," but rather as a "designer" who uses many resources—including typography—as a means to solve visual communication problems. His attraction to typography as a versatile tool for design began during his early days as a student, and evolved into an area of critical focus as a graduate student at Yale. Geismar's Master's thesis included a written history of sans serif typefaces and the design of a new face.

His development as a designer has been most influenced by the Yale faculty and fellow students, especially **Josef Albers** and his partner **Robert Brownjohn,** in the first years of practice. Other influences have also served as a catalyst for his own thinking. "The generation of **Beall, Lustig, Brodovitch, Rand, Bayer** had the greatest influence for me. But," he states, "I am attracted to many approaches, from the vigor of late 19th century typographic posters to the 'neue grafik' of **Max Bill** and Hans Neuberg."

In 1957, the firm of Brownjohn, Chermayeff & Geismar was founded (**Ivan Chermayeff** had been a classmate of Geismar at Yale). Geismar and his partners instituted a new approach to design—rooted in the **Bauhaus**—that approached problem solving from a wide range of design areas. Because of the diversity of their work, they preferred to call their firm a "design office" rather than an "art studio." They were approaching design as it had never been done before in America. Of their widespread activities, **Gene Federico** said: "It is evident . . . they are well versed in this 'language' of today, and they use it with virtuosity. Moreover, there is more than a suggestion that they have

1   Cover for a press kit for Fox Theaters.

2   Title page for an alphabet book entitled *26 Tales of Woe.*

already perceived some of tomorrow's 'sounds'."
In 1960, with the departure of Brownjohn
to England, the firm became the well-known
Chermayeff and Geismar. Associates.

For nearly thirty years, this firm has adhered to
a consistent philosophy, enabling it to keep
pace with the times. Solutions, emerging from
the problems themselves, take into consideration social and cultural changes, automatically
rejecting the arbitrary application of style
and fashion. The wide range of design activities
in which this firm engages includes corporate
identification, exhibitions, packaging, and
architectural graphics.

Whether Geismar is involved with corporate
identification programs (he has been responsible
for over a hundred of these, including Xerox,
Seatrain Lines, Brentano's, and Best Products),
exhibition designs, or other graphic design
applications, his concern is with the simplicity,
clarity, and accuracy of message transmission.
These concerns are represented in his logotype
designs, Mobil Oil being an effective example

Thomas H. Geismar (born in 1932 in

Glen Ridge, New Jersey) is a Partner

in the firm of Chermayeff and Geis-

mar Associates in New York City.

He received a BA degree from Brown

University in 1953 and an MFA in

Graphic Design at Yale in 1958. He

has received wide acclaim for the

design of numerous corporate identity

programs and exhibitions. His work

has been exhibited throughout the

world, and he has received major

awards from many professional or-

ganizations, including the American

Institute of Graphic Arts Gold Medal

in 1979.

6   5

3–5   Logotypes for Xerox Corporation,
       Mobil Oil, and Seatrain Lines.

6   Book jacket for *AIGA Graphic
       Design USA:1.*

Thomas H. Geismar

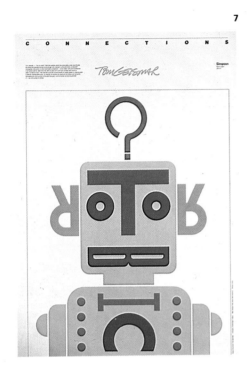

(Fig. 4). Composed of only five vertical strokes, two circular forms, and the angle of the *M*, this trademark is a memorable configuration because of its startling simplicity. His symbol design for the fiftieth anniversary of The Museum of Modern Art contains only three contrasting shapes whose arrangement implies both the spatial interaction of abstract forms in a painting and the number *50* (Fig. 8). As seen in this example, Geismar is able to transform a few carefully chosen and placed forms into multi-layered typographic signs. The full range of applications within his corporate identification programs is approached with the same economy of means and attention to detail.

One senses, in viewing Geismar's typographic work, a commitment to exploration. He often fuses type, found objects, and a variety of invented signs into collages that challenge a viewer into active participation. His design

for Simpson Paper Company's *Connection* series demonstrates this point by making a statement about the ability of the human mind to make illogical connections, and the inability for the "mind" of a machine to do the same. A viewer sees both an image of a robot and the word *robotic* through the interaction of contrasting letterforms (Fig. 7). This concept is reminiscent of the "masks" created by **Bradbury Thompson** for *Westvaco Inspirations*.

The projects that appeal most to Geismar are those "in which the designer is able to control the content, to make a significant contribution to the concept and direction of the project. . . . While I enjoy the 'craft' aspect of design and typography," he says, "it is the conceptual part that occupies more and more of my time and energy."

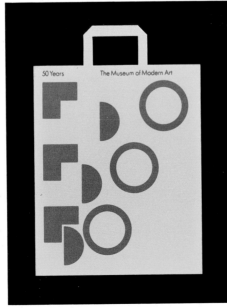

7   One of a series of posters for Simpson Paper.

8   Shopping bag for the fiftieth anniversary of the Museum of Modern Art.

9   Construction fence for Tishman-Speyer, New York City.

10   Cover for first *AIGA Journal*.

11   Poster for Designer's Saturday.

Designer's
Saturday
New York
Oct 7-8

GEISMAR

Geismar's exploration of the language of typography has remained as steadfast today as it was in 1959 when he and his colleagues wrote: "In the area of typography we have felt, as other more experienced designers have demonstrated, that the mere use of typographic elements arranged in space is frequently insufficient as a means of communicating whatever messages we are limited to at a given moment. We are in continual search for a wider vocabulary. Not newer typefaces and new graphic methods, although they are always welcome, but new ways of approach, and new ways of seeing. Not new for newness' sake, but to give vitality to ideas rather than to promote private and personal visual expressions."

Diana Graham

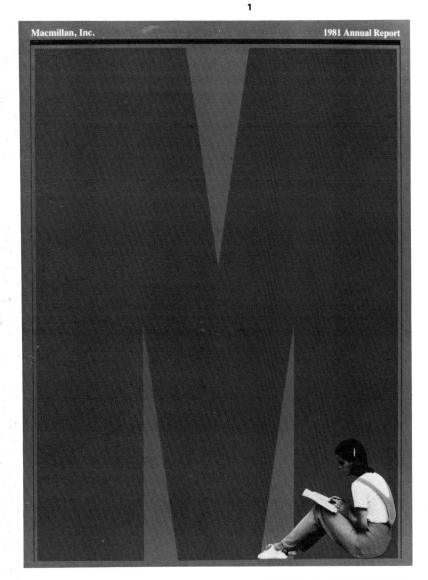

1

Macmillan, Inc.   1981 Annual Report

2

---

1 Annual report cover for Macmillan, Inc. Photograph by Tom Zimberhoff.

2 Page from *A Twenty-four Page Book*, New York Art Director's Club. Co-designed with Wing Chan and Ivy Li.

As an Air Force brat, Diana Graham lived in many different places as a child, including Japan, Spain, Mississippi, and California. This nomadic upbringing provided her with a strong sense of individuality, a need for constant variety, and the ability to adapt to any situation.

In 1961, she settled in New York City, attended Christopher Columbus High School in the Bronx, and went on to the School of Visual Arts for training in design. Her first job, in the office of **George Tscherny,** she obtained after he saw a TV title comp she had designed in an SVA class. Tscherny saw much potential in it, turning away three other SVA portfolios in favor of Graham's sketch. For Tscherny, Graham did *exactly* as she was told, realizing that she could learn much from one of the great leaders in the industry. Working on mechanicals and tediously positioning adhesive films to comprehensives, she developed a high degree of craftsmanship, accuracy, and discipline.

Graham acquired two other skills by working professionally with her former SVA teachers, Roger Ferriter and Phil Gips. Ferriter shared his expertise in typography, helping her to realize that the medium could be simultaneously functional and beautiful. Gips taught her that she could safely "stray from the use of the grid," and that *ideas* are what really matter.

Others have also had their effect upon Graham, but if she were to choose one designer that has influenced her the most, it would be **Paul Rand.** Referring to him as "an icon of graphic design," she recognizes his role in pioneering a modern approach to visual problem solving.

It would be difficult to trace an evolution in Graham's work, for she does not work within a specific style. Because she allows problems to dictate solutions, and responds to many ideas, her work appears infinitely varied. She also works on a wide range of projects—from corporate design to movie logos and posters, environmental graphics, exhibits, and packages. There are attributes within her work, however, that bring unity to the diversity.

3

5

Diana Graham (born in 1944 in Denver, Colorado) is President of Diagram Design and Marketing Communications, Inc. She graduated from the School of Visual Arts, New York, in 1965. She has distinguished herself with numerous national and international design awards, including the International Designer of the Year Award for Women in Design. Her work has been featured in *Novum Gebrauchsgraphik*, *Communication Arts* magazine, *Graphic Design: New York*, and *Graphics USA*.

Perhaps the most recognizable of these is the directness of her approach. Type and image in simple compositions say precisely what needs to be said for effective communication. Typefaces are chosen for their ability to carry a message: "I generate many, many rough tissues of different typefaces. I examine these in terms of the overall problem, and this establishes the criteria for selection."

While her solutions are clean, simple, and effective, they also possess a "poetic" quality. The visual elements of her compositions—their arrangement, scale, color, texture, and inter-relationships—are not merely proxies for products and services; they possess a value and meaning of their own. Posters for Mobil Oil, for example, are recognized for their intrinsic beauty as well as for their role in communication (Figs. 7, 8). The *Norway* poster introduces a large letter *N*, defined and dramatized by two counterforms appearing as figures on the ground. The geometrical quality of the poster is accentuated by the curving hull of a Viking ship moving through the bottom counterform.

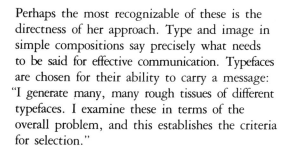

6

3   Poster for an avant-garde dance group.

4–6   Logotypes for Diagram Design and Marketing Communications, Inc.; New England Petroleum Company; Del Rey, a paperback book publisher.

Diana Graham

In Japan's highly competitive market for petroleum products, Mobil Sekiyu K.K. holds a 5 percent share. With interests in four refineries, Mobil Sekiyu emphasizes gasoline and diesel oil, home heating fuels, heavy fuels and lube oils. An LPG import terminal with storage capacity of 180,000 metric tons was completed in 1981 in an affiliated refinery, and Mobil Sekiyu K.K. has started large volume import of LPG from the Middle East.

Mobil companies are good customers of Japanese shipbuilders. They took delivery of seven tankers in 1982, and will add another to the Mobil fleet in 1983. Moreover, Mobil Search, the world's largest and most advanced seismic vessel, was built in Japan and will be in operation in 1983.

The need for energy is worldwide.
So are Mobil's efforts to help meet it.

Mobil

The poetic quality of her work is also demonstrated in a page for a book dedicated to the design of novelty page numbers (Fig. 2). For page twelve, Graham placed several brightly colored shapes on the contours of darker, bolder forms. The incompletion of this typographic image enables a reader to perceive it either as pure abstract form or as the number *12*.

Graham relies upon intuition to solve visual problems, stating that "Ideas can come from anywhere, anytime, anything. It's totally unexpected. I believe that we, as designers, are collectors of information. Everywhere I go, everything I do and see contributes information to my world of experiences so that when I approach a problem, the idea emerges from an intuitive feeling."

Rudolf Arnheim, in *Visual Thinking*, helps us to understand two approaches to perceptual thinking: intuitive and intellectual. "The components of intuitive thought processes," he says, "interact within a continuous field. Those of intellectual processes follow each other in linear succession." In other words, intuitive problem solving is made possible by thought mechanisms that establish relationships between parts within a whole. Intellectual problem solving isolates parts, collects data on each, and combines them into logical and stable structures.

Graham's ability to synthesize the usual polarities in design—form vs. function, beauty vs. utility, and rational vs. irrational—is an indication that she employs aspects of both intuitive and intellectual problem solving. Henri Poincare said: "It is by logic that we prove, but by intuition that we discover."

7,8   **Posters for Mobil Oil.**

9,10   **Booklet for the opening of Diagram Design and Marketing Communications, Inc. Co-designed by Wing Chan.**

In Norway, Mobil Exploration Norway, Inc., is operator, for itself and its partners, of the Statfjord field, the largest oil field discovered in the North Sea, and soon to be the most productive.

With average daily production of 300,000 barrels of oil and 275 million cubic feet of natural gas, the Statfjord A platform will soon be joined by Statfjord B, the most advanced concrete platform ever built. A third platform, Statfjord C, is now under construction. All are Mobil engineered. By 1986, production in the Statfjord field is expected to range from 500,000 to 600,000 barrels a day. Mobil's share is 12.61 percent.

Mobil Oil A/S Norge markets petroleum products in Norway, with emphasis on automotive fuels and lubricants, and home heating fuel.

The need for energy is worldwide. So are Mobil's efforts to help meet it.

Mobil®

Malcolm Grear

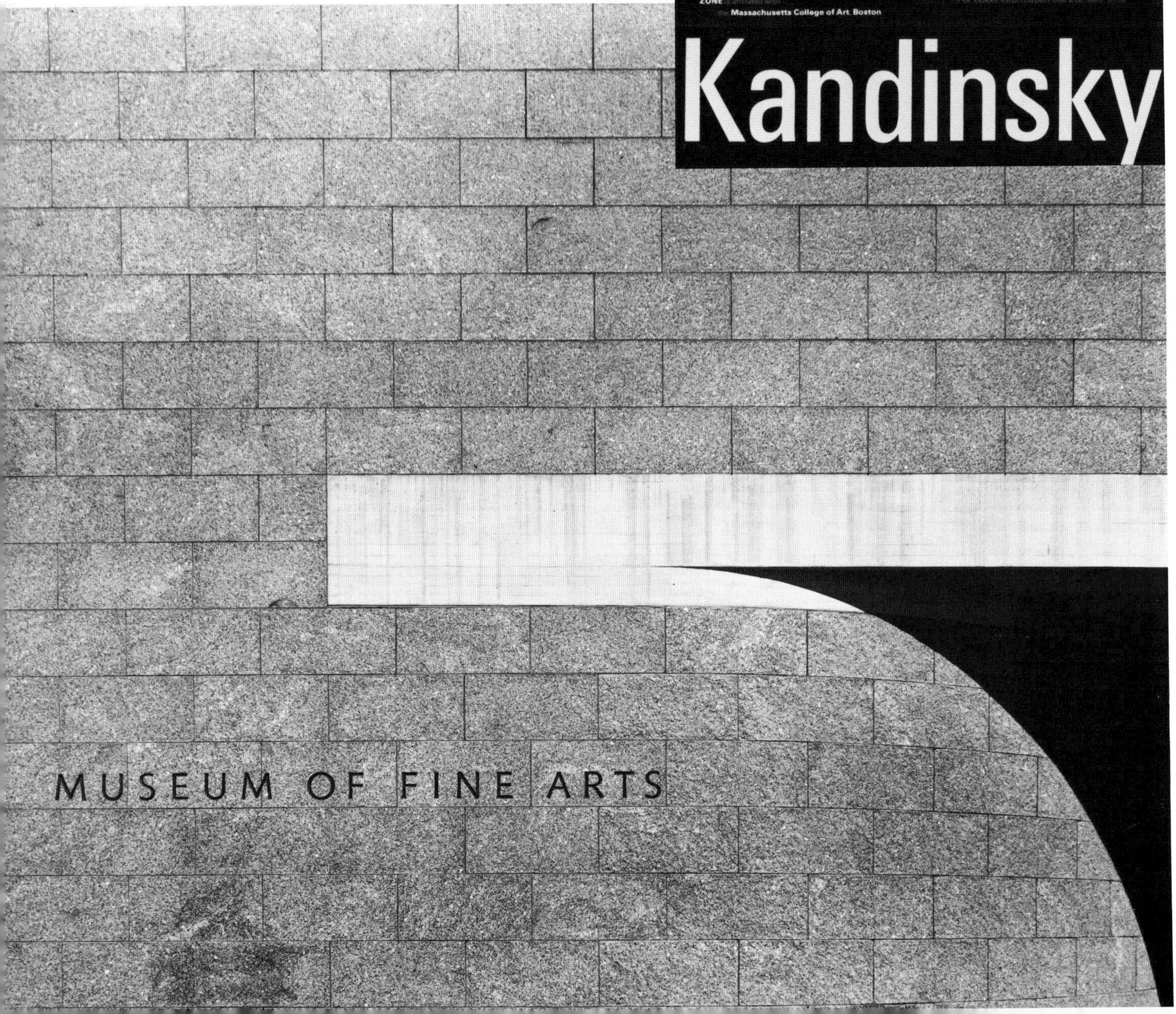

2

1 Exterior sign for the Boston Museum
   of Fine Arts. Architecture:
   I. M. Pei and Partners.

ZONE

Theater of the **Visual**
directed by **Harris** and **Ros Barron**
presents its adaptation of

**Vasily Kandinsky's
The Yellow Sound**

The **Solomon R. Guggenheim Museum**
1071 Fifth Avenue, New York City
Opening **May 12**, 1972 for a limited run
Performances at **8:30** pm Tuesday—Sunday
Special benefit performance **May 11**, 1972
For ticket information call 212-369-5710

Performances supported
by the **New York Foundation
for the Arts, Inc.** with funds provided
by the **New York State Council on the Arts**
ZONE is affiliated with
the **Massachusetts College of Art, Boston**

Kandinsky

MUSEUM OF FINE ARTS

Malcolm Grear was born in the backwoods of Kentucky. He is a witty, intelligent, sophisticated, yet "down-home" designer. He first became acquainted with letterforms while a young high school student working as a sign painter after school and during the weekends. For a year after leaving high school, he operated a successful sign shop, and for four years after enlisting in the Navy as a metalsmith, he worked as a part-time sign painter. After the Navy, Grear found his way to the Art Academy of Cincinnati, where one of the school's teachers, **Noel Martin,** instilled in him a love for typography. Appropriately, Grear describes Martin as being his "typographical Johnny Appleseed."

While at the Academy, Grear earnestly sought to weave design history and studio courses into the heart of his design education. Now, as a professor at the Rhode Island School of Design and principal of Malcolm Grear Designers in Providence, Rhode Island, he finds it difficult to imagine life without design history. He has been inspired by the legacies of **Guillaume Apollinaire, Lewis Carroll, Piet Zwart, Kurt Schwitters,** and **Jan Tschichold.** More recent typographers, however, have had the greatest impact on him—such people as Noel Martin, **Norman Ives,** and **Bradbury Thompson.** Grear can appreciate the integrity of the work of these and other typographic designers without necessarily liking their visual approaches.

He resists falling into stylistic traps. He believes vehemently and declares passionately that "typography transcends style." Therefore, he opens his senses to other art forms. Painting, sculpture, architecture, poetry, and music, each in its own way brings life to his work. He believes that good typography, the most powerful and potent typography, is based upon a careful balancing act: discipline balanced with freedom, information with inspiration, and skills with ideas. Typography must always perform its task; it must give order to information. This, above anything else, is at the center of Grear's design philosophy and is the basis for his work.

3

The Guggenheim Museum

4

Malcolm Grear (born in 1931 in Mill Spring, Kentucky) is President of Malcolm Grear Designers, Inc., and Professor of Graphic Design at the Rhode Island School of Design. He was educated at the Art Academy of Cincinnati, Ohio. For his work in graphic design, he has received many awards from such organizations as the American Institute of Graphic Arts, the International Center for the Typographic Arts, and the Art Society of North America. He has lectured throughout the United States and his work has been published in such distinguished journals as *Signs/Signet/Symbol, Typomundus 20,* and *Contemporary Designers.*

2 Poster for a performance at the Guggenheim Museum.

3,4 Symbols for the Guggenheim Museum, and Providence Journal Company.

Malcolm Grear

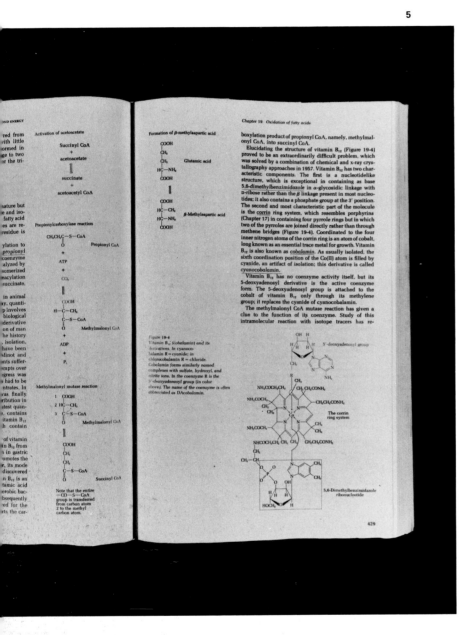

As President of Malcolm Grear Designers, Inc., Grear oversees all projects that enter the studio. However, he sensitively acknowledges the important role of each designer on his staff. A wide variety of projects, from large-scale environmental projects to posters occupy the studio's drawing boards.

Grear is a classicist whose work reveals a consistent respect for time-honored typefaces and their studied application to space. Yet for him, some old design truths have fallen by the wayside. Experience has taught him to look at typographic "rules" objectively, to smile at many of them, to break and bend others. It is in this context that he feels fortunate to have had an American typographic upbringing: "I am able to look at what has been done to serve as a springboard instead of being strapped with a heritage of rules, not to be broken."

Grear's typography transcends the mundane arrangements of forms on two-dimensional surfaces. Letterforms and their positions are chosen for the purpose of making clear statements. Sometimes, he will spend hours choosing the right typeface for a particular situation. Before a decision is made about which typeface to use, he will consider design, readability, weight, harmony, and the classical qualities inherent in a face; if he feels that the ascenders or descenders are not right, or that there is a buildup of color in the wrong places, he will go on to something else. This attitude translates into a diverse body of work that ranges from the simple and elegant to the gutsy and dramatic.

The sensitivity that Grear brings to his typographic design is revealed in the design of a biochemistry textbook (Fig. 5). Using beautiful Renaissance proportions to present complex scientific information, he places a single readable column of text type within generous margins. Accompanying these margins are masterfully composed diagrams—too many to count—that simplify the task of understanding difficult abstract concepts.

5   Interior spread from a biochemistry textbook.

6   Logotype for Brown
University Press.

7   Poster for an international sculpture exhibition.

8   Catalog cover for a Miro exhibition
at the Guggenheim Museum.

6

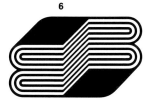

The diversity of Grear's typographic design is represented in a dynamic and experimental catalog cover for a Miro exhibition at the Guggenheim Museum (Fig. 8). On wispy sprays of white, letterforms are stencilled, distorted, and angled as if on a Miro canvas: free and childlike. Such wide diversity is characteristic of Grear's work, and reveals his preference for communication over imitation.

Grear's concern for clear communication is heightened by the current fury of technological change. He expresses restrained optimism about the future of typography in light of this change: "There is little doubt that the concerns of serious typographic designers will eventually be eliminated; but for the present period of development, the universal language of typographers has been fragmented, partly because of the speedy pace of development and the competitiveness of the companies trying to keep their instructional language specific to their equipment." The result of this dilemma is an outpouring of typefaces for the computer, typefaces so poorly drawn that they no longer resemble original cuts. Grear aptly compares it to putting plastic siding that simulates wooden clapboards on beautiful New England houses. He continues: "Some classic faces are so poorly translated, transferred or distorted that they are barely recognizable. . . . For the most part, the new typefaces that are being designed today try to 'out ugly each other.' They are trendy and are forced to look 'chic.' "

Obviously, Grear speaks his mind. This quality of straightforwardness is not only at the center of his exemplary work, but is also at the heart of his personality. He emerged from America's rural interior an earthy, distinguished innovator, one whose design view has vitalized and humanized the profession.

7

8

April Greiman

Greiman is the ultimate risktaker. In 1986, she was asked by the Walker Art Center to do an issue of *Design Quarterly* featuring her work. She decided that it should involve her investigations of the Macintosh computer. The format of the publication was left to Greiman's imagination, and her solution was one that very few designers would seriously consider as a possibility. The magazine took the form of a 25½″ × 76½″ broadside folded into twenty-one panels (forty-two pages), placed into a standard-sized folder. Featured on one side of this enormous sheet of paper is a life-size, nude, digitized image of Greiman. This is layered with dozens of smaller images, typographical notations, and ideograms about the creation of man. While markedly self-indulgent, the piece nonetheless is a tribute to Greiman's self-assurance and adventurous spirit. The signature line of the piece reads, "made in space by April Greiman."

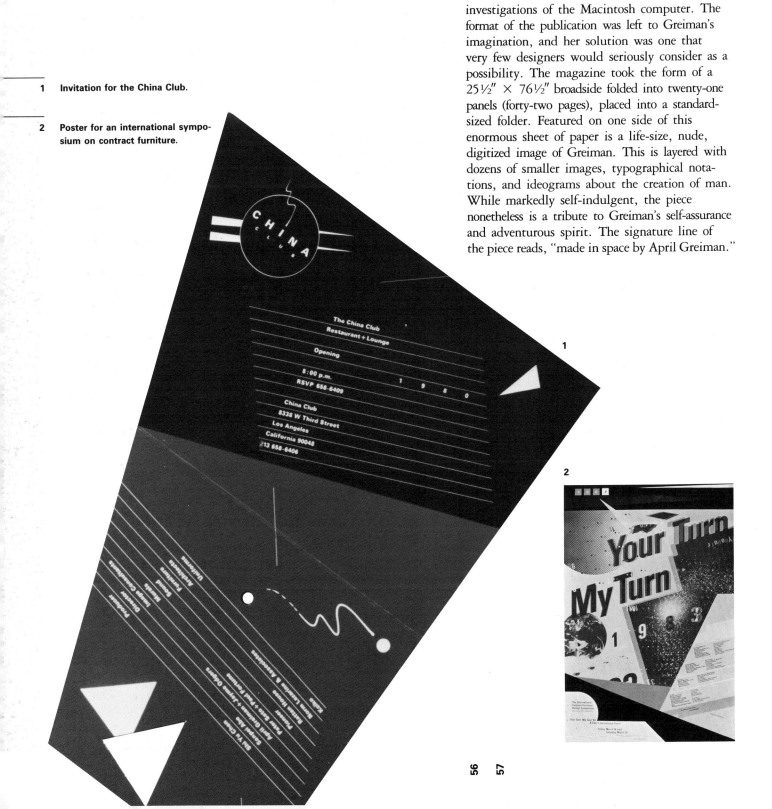

1

2

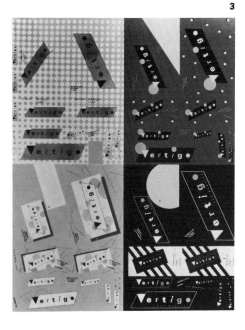
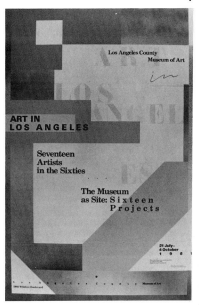

April Greiman (born in 1948 in New York City) is President of April Greiman Incorporated, Los Angeles. She received a BFA in design from the Kansas City Art Institute in 1970 and studied at the Allgemeine Kunstgewerbeschule, Basel from 1970–71. Her work is widely published and exhibited throughout the world. Publications include *Seven Graphic Designers*, Tokyo; and *A History of Graphic Design*. She has received numerous awards from the major design organizations, and she lectures regularly throughout the United States.

Originally from New York, Greiman began her study of design at the Kansas City Art Institute, where she came under the influence of visiting Swiss designers teaching in the program. These teachers had such a profound impact upon Greiman that upon graduation she immediately enrolled at the **Allgemeine Kunstgewerbeschule** (the School of Design) in Basel for a year of study. While at Basel, the writings of **Emil Ruder** and the teachings of **Armin Hofmann** and **Wolfgang Weingart** became the nucleus of her own investigations. From Hofmann she assimilated the need to examine the communicative potential of abstract and elemental form; from Weingart, a tireless experimenter, she learned to defiantly question time-honored traditions of typography and to view anything "new" as passé. Of the many things she learned at Basel, it was perhaps Weingart's unique attitudes towards form and communication, and his bent for breaking the "rules" that affected her the most. This influence remains visibly apparent in her work.

Upon returning to the United States from Basel, Greiman divided her time between teaching and professional practice. In 1976 she settled in Los Angeles, a city that matched her exotic temperament. Upon her arrival, key clients

3   Promotional poster for Vertigo.

4   Poster for an exhibition at the Los Angeles County Museum of Art.

April Greiman

such as *Wet* magazine and The California Institute of the Arts gave her free rein to explore new ideas. The work produced for these clients brought immediate national attention, for it was a daring approach that had not yet been experienced in America.

As other American designers trained in Swiss methods began to enlarge their formal vocabulary, a new trend in graphic design emerged. It was given the label **"Post-Modernism."** Wolfgang Weingart is directly linked to this development, for his work ten years earlier had already explored much of what was now just beginning to happen in America. When his American students arrived back in the States, they brought his influence with them, but broadened it. Greiman added a new dimension to her Basel training with a powerful sense of visual drama, fresh conception of form and space, and ingenious use of color and photography.

Other developments occurred in American design—particularly in architecture—that set the stage for Post-Modern graphic design. Beginning in the mid–1960s, architects began to apply ornament to the surfaces of their buildings in response to more than a generation of high-rise glass boxes. **Robert Venturi,** one of the earliest of these architects, reacted to **Mies van der Rohe's** dictum "less is more" with "less is a bore." Ornament was applied to surfaces not only to satisfy a basic human desire, but also because it was capable of functioning as a language of form that places an object in time and reveals its purpose. Because graphic design and typography are the most ephemeral and fast-changing of the design disciplines, developments in these areas often follow on the heels of major changes in architecture.

Greiman transforms two-dimensional typographic pages into dynamic, three-dimensional spaces somewhat reminiscent of the **Proun** paintings by **El Lissitzky.** Typography, abstract geometrical forms, linear elements, and gestural shapes combine with psychedelic color and vivid texture to fool the eye, to shock, and to surprise the viewer with an ambiguous reality. Linear elements suggesting perspective; trapezoidal shapes hovering in space; drop shadows suggesting light sources; and graphic elements set against wide-angle, expansive photographs are part of this lexicon of form. An early example of her work, the *Cal Arts Viewbook* produced in 1979, presents a dynamic medley of brightly colored forms that float aimlessly, weaving in and out of a black spatial field (Fig. 6). One of these forms—a Polaroid photograph of palm trees, sky, and clouds—not only signifies sunny California, but also a window into another space and time.

More recently, Greiman has explored the potential of layered information. Her work in this area is closely related to experiments initiated by Wolfgang Weingart in the mid-1970s. Using film positives, Weingart overlapped images, type, and textures to create complex fields of visual information. Greiman uses electronic tools to produce similar results; however, her textured layerings are digitally produced, having a quality reflective of the technology. Her cover design for *PC World* magazine is an example of this work (Fig. 8).

The Macintosh computer is one of Greiman's most significant tools. She finds it to be "accessible yet subtle at the same time, based on a highly 'physical', intuitive, visual, 'iconic' language for the user." She uses this tool both in the early and the late stages of the design process. It has been applied to graphic design as well as to the design of furniture, interiors, and fabrics. For Greiman, the Macintosh "contradicts and in fact resolves the usual dualities: right/left brain, loose/tight, man/ machine, thinking/feeling." The responsive character of this machine suits her well, for her design sensibility continually travels back and forth between visual order and chaos.

April Greiman is one of the most influential and controversial of America's contemporary designers. With one foot in the future, she consistently sends shockwaves through the design establishment with her unorthodox and progressive approach to design.

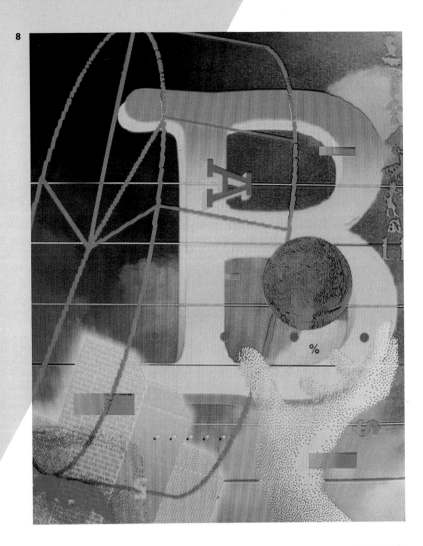

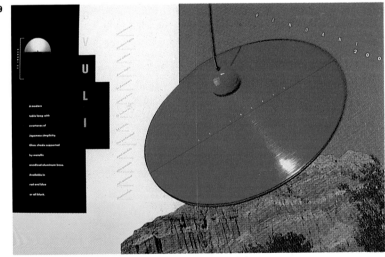

8 Cover for *PC World* magazine.

9 Interior spread from a brochure for Ron Resek Lighting and Furniture.

Willi Kunz

1

Fredrich Cantor

strange VICISSITUDES

June 17
July 8
   78

FOTO
492 Broome Street
New York, NY 10013

2

ROME

Photographs by
Fredrich Cantor

July 10
August 5
1978

Sheldon Memorial Art Gallery
University of Nebraska
Lincoln, Nebraska

In a 1978 edition of the *AIGA Journal*, an article describes the publishers of **Print** magazine opening their office mail one afternoon. Among the samples of graphic design, they saw something for the first time. Rose DeNeve, former managing editor of the magazine, describes the event: "The whole gestalt of the piece was something we hadn't seen before . . . it combined two photographs of unequal sizes with several lines of type of unequal weights. Some of the type was tilted at an angle across the page, slicing right through the larger photograph. Here and there were some fat black bands, and all of these elements seemed to float on a sea of polka dots. We didn't know it at the time, but we were looking at the leading edge of what some have called a whole new movement in graphic design, embodied in a poster that has since been hailed as a quintessential example of **Post-Modern** design." This poster was for an exhibition of photographs by Fredrich Cantor (Fig. 1). The designer is Willi Kunz.

Kunz began preparation for a professional career in typography by serving a four-year compositor's apprenticeship in Switzerland. The vocational school that he attended included classes in typographic design, and he soon realized that he was motivated in the area of design rather than in the purely technical aspects of typesetting. Upon graduating with a national diploma, he decided to pursue studies in graphic design at the **Allgemeine Kunstgewerbeschule** (the School of Design) in Basel.

Here, Kunz studied with **Emil Ruder, Armin Hofmann,** and Hans Rudolf Bosshard. He has since established a highly personal approach to design, but the timeless principles of Swiss objectivity that he learned from his teachers— Ruder's call for a balance between form and function, and the need for a systematic, structural approach to design; and Hofmann's quest for a visual language based upon form—have remained an integral part of his work.

Two early innovators of modern typography have also had a significant impact upon his work: **Piet Zwart,** the Dutch "Typotekt" (typographic designer and architect) affiliated with the

de Stijl movement, who constructed the well-known NKF ads and catalogs; and **Jan Tschichold,** the leading advocate of the "New Typography," who said: "The new typography is not a fashion." Kunz similarly believes that "effective typography must communicate the message and not style."

Kunz's process has changed over the years from typographic to the more visual and expressive "typo-graphic." Complex fields of type, rules, photographs, and abstract shapes are combined, shifted, split, stepped, and layered—challenging the eye to travel through visual constellations of beauty and order. Rarely does Kunz use a predetermined structure, such as a grid, as the basis for his typographic work. He "builds" compositions from the functional requirements of the communication, and from the specific visual characteristics of type and image.

Structure is never arbitrary; it is an integral part of the message. In a poster for an exhibition, he uses a photograph of classical architectural forms to establish structure (Fig. 2). These forms—consisting of columns and steps appearing in a grid-like pattern—are reinterpreted as a series of simple geometric shapes. These both establish an orderly framework for the poster

Willi Kunz (born in Switzerland) is

the Principal in the firm of Willi Kunz

Associates Inc., New York City. He

served a four-year occupational

apprenticeship receiving a Swiss

National Diploma, and studied and

taught at the Allgemeine Kunst-

gewerbeschule in Basel. His dis-

tinguished work has been featured

in such design publications as *Typo-

graphische Monatsblaetter, Octavo,*

and *Typographic Design: Form and

Communication*; and it has been

exhibited throughout the United

States, Europe, and Japan.

3

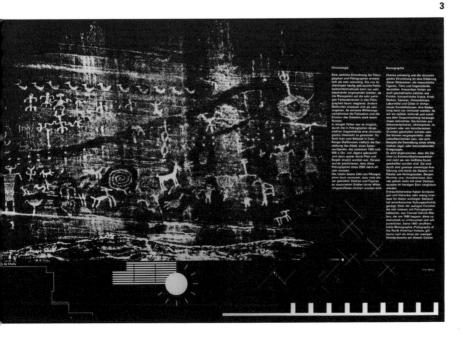

1,2   Posters for exhibitions of photographs by Fredrich Cantor.

3   Interior spread about petroglyphs from *Typographische Monatsblaetter.*

4 Poster announcing a study program
in New York and Paris sponsored
by the Columbia University
School of Architecture, Planning,
and Preservation.

5 Cover from a type specimen
book on Univers for Typogram,
New York.

Typogram

Univers

An overview
of Univers typefaces
from Typogram.

Univers 39
Univers 45
Univers 46
Univers 47
Univers 48
Univers 49
Univers 53
Univers 55
Univers 56
Univers 57
Univers 58
Univers 59
Univers 63
Univers 65
Univers 66
Univers 67
Univers 68
Univers 73
Univers 75
Univers 76
Univers 83
Univers 85

Typogram
900 Broadway
New York, NY 10003
212 505 1640
800 USA TYPE

and mimic the composition and visual qualities of the photograph. A hierarchical corridor of type is unified with the image.

According to Kunz, creative solutions to typographic problems can only be achieved by working with the actual typographic materials. Only by this means can the sensitive designer understand the syntactical aspects of a message. He elaborates upon this process: "I generally do not spend a significant amount of time on sketches. After organizing my ideas I proceed with ordering the basic design components from my typographic supplier. The final solution usually evolves from a broad exploration which requires many adjustments in typesetting."

Kunz is an "information architect" who uses the time-tested principles of visual syntax to explore new ideas, to find order amidst confusion, and to inspire future design directions. "The syntactical dimension of typography still presents designers with limitless potential for exploration and the development of exciting visual results. But the first step is the realization that the essential qualities and strength of typographic design lie primarily in its structure and not in any particular typeface. In fact the typeface should be as unobtrusive as possible. Good typographic design is always a critical interpretation of a message, and the consideration of form and structure an integral part of the process."

6   Typographic design for an oil
     container for Merit.

7,8 Posters for the *Wednesday
     Lecture Series*, Columbia University
     School of Architecture, Planning,
     and Preservation.

Warren Lehrer

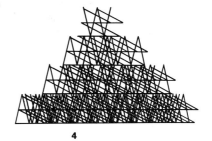

4

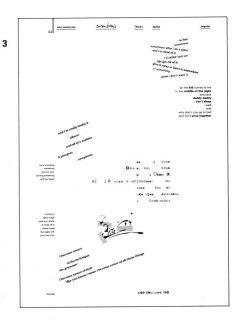

During a critique of his work while in college, Warren Lehrer boldly showed his professor a secret drawing composed entirely of invented words and other markings. The professor shook his head—sorely dismayed by obviously misguided talent—and told him that he should *never* for any reason make pictures with letterforms, or combine words with images. Lehrer knew instantly that he had received a calling in life, a sacred mission.

A few years later, an informed and inspired professor introduced Lehrer to concrete poetry, the books of **Diter Rot,** as well as the collages of **Kurt Schwitters** and **Norman Ives.** He also urged Lehrer to pursue graduate study in graphic design at Yale to complement his growing obsession for experimental typography. "At the time," Lehrer explains, "I perceived graphic design to be an avant-garde field of artistic research into a kind of abstract visual language. I eventually realized that my involvement with typography was practically the opposite to that of most graphic designers, in that being a writer, I cared for and had control of my text, had nothing to sell, no client to second guess, in addition to possessing a sensibility obsessed with the complex and the subtle."

1

2   3

1–3   Pages from *i mean you know.*

4   Construction from the limited-edition book *Type Dreams.*

Lehrer is a multi-disciplinary artist (writer, performer, composer, book artist, and designer). He is involved with the creation of works that juxtapose human characters within musical and theatrical settings. In his books he uses typography as a means of making narrative language visible. These intriguing books are studies in human dialogue and the poetics of communication. To fully appreciate Lehrer's books, readers must suspend preconceptions about how books are to be read; for his defy tradition, redefining both form and function. Lehrer's page spreads serve as stages for the characters of his books, enabling readers to participate in the drama by determining the pacing and the order of events.

i mean you know, written and designed by Lehrer, functions both as a book to be approached creatively by the reader, and as a script or score to be used for a performance (Figs. 1–3). The setting of the book is a building with translucent walls that form visible but illusive barriers between the seven characters. This enables the reader to eavesdrop on all of them at the same time.

The characters in Lehrer's books are developed by making "psycho-acoustic" translations of text. This is a process by which fictional characters are "typecast" into typefaces, typographic arrangements, and colors reflective of their personalities. Each voice is seen just as it might be heard in the course of normal conversation, for the properties of the text determine the form. Spatial intervals between letters, words, and lines are adjusted to the natural cadence of speech, and the repetition of words and phrases intensify the reader's perceptions of each character. Conversations, often layered and mixed and occurring simultaneously, angle their way into the page, turn, shift in confusion, and angle off again.

Two of the characters in *i mean you know*— Trombonio and Violone—express themselves in musical notation rather than words, demonstrating the communicative potential of abstract form. A third character is Little Tracy, whose verbal/visual babblings are set in four weights of

5

Warren Lehrer (born in 1955 in New York City) is the Director of The Center for Editions and Professor of Design at SUNY Purchase. He received a BA degree in painting from Queens College in 1977 and an MFA degree in Graphic Design at Yale in 1980. In 1978 he established Ear/Say, a workshop involved in small press publishing, writing, performance, audio composition, and design. He has performed and exhibited throughout the United States and Europe, and has received awards from such organizations as the American Institute of Graphic Arts, the Type Directors Club, and the National Endowment for the Arts.

5 Announcement for a letterpress book workshop.

Warren Lehrer

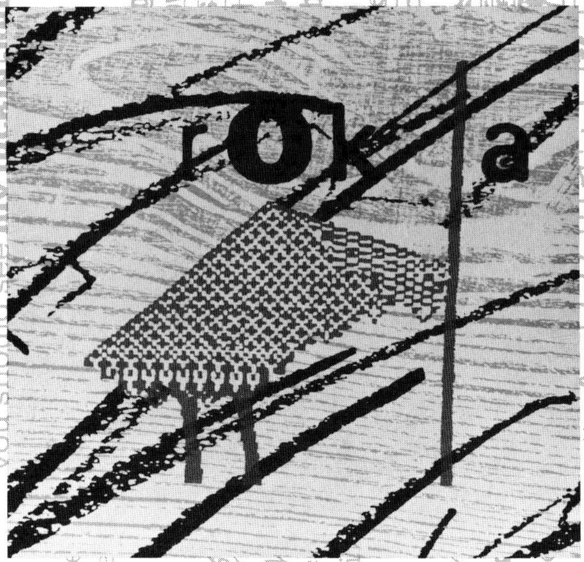

Univers revealing a spontaneous, unpredictable, and erratic infant. Other characters include Ace Monroe, a smooth talking disc-jockey whose even, upbeat, and confident voice is consistently angled upward in Zapf bold and bold italic; and Angelica, a sixty-year-old black house painter from Alabama who has lived in the North for almost forty years. She speaks a kind of southern dialect in Jan Baker Lowercase Bounce, an animated handwriting.

Other typographic and spatial cues echo the subtle qualities of spoken language and are woven into the conversational framework: as time passes, type moves from the top of pages to the bottom; line endings serve as punctuation indicating slight breath pauses; two or more characters appearing on the same horizontal axis are read simultaneously; and typographic size or weight change represents increased or decreased volume.

In *French Fries*, a book that is also a play and a metaphor for life, Lehrer presents a group portrait set in the Dream Queen restaurant (Figs. 9–12). It is "a quick service circus of culinary discourse, argument, memory, dream, loss and twisted aspiration." Once into the book (which is packaged as an oversize order of French fries) the reader is guided through the back door of the restaurant into a dynamic world of type, images, pictographs, and symbols. An oblique cast of characters, unaware of the reader's presence, include eight regulars, Flash (a psychotic supermarket of fast-food personalities), and the voices of six more characters

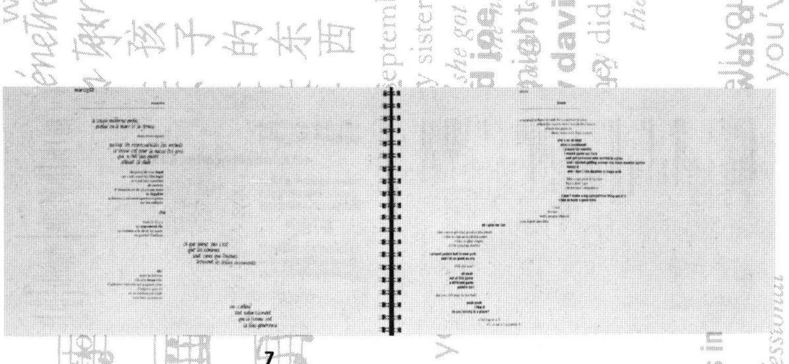

6

7

8

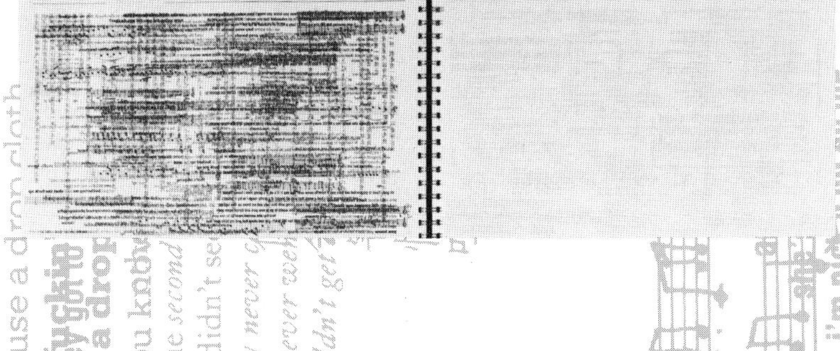

6   **Page from *Grrr*.**

7,8   **Interior spreads from *Versations*.**

10

9

heard over boom boxes brought in by the customers. Everything from religion to politics to the virtues of the potato in America are discussed, argued, and tossed around at the Dream Queen. The book reaches a startling crescendo when in the course of a political discussion, all hell breaks loose, and the pages accelerate into a cacophony of visual sounds.

Translating the spoken word into the visual word is not new. It is rooted in several historical experiments, and Lehrer has ingeniously extended earlier efforts by exploring the most subtle nuances of the genre. His influences are broad-based and include among others the illuminated manuscripts of the Middle Ages and the lyricism of ancient Greek poetry. While reading Lehrer's books, one might think of **Robert Massin's** interpretations of Ionesco's *The Bald Soprano* (see Page 136 in Major Resources); the textural, musical writings of **Gertrude Stein;** or the typographic performances of **John Cage.** The visual interpretations of sound, characteristic of **Futurism** and **Dada,** and the work of innovative concrete poets such as **e.e. cummings** resonate throughout Lehrer's work.

Fortunately, while in college, Lehrer didn't lower his head and follow his professor's advice to abandon his penchant for invented words in his paintings. His defiance of "rules" and established traditions has led him to new and adventurous modes of typographic expression and communication.

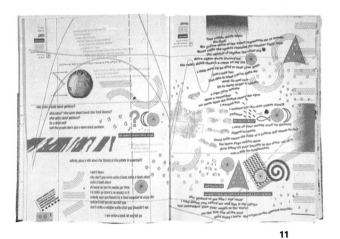

11

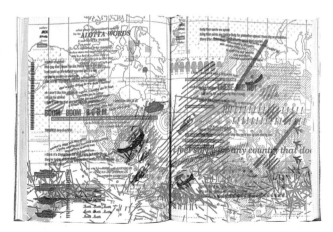

12

9–12 **Cover and interior spreads from**
French Fries.

Michael Manwaring

3

4

Michael Manwaring (born in 1942 in
Palo Alto, California) studied design,
painting, and etching at the San
Francisco Art Institute. The Office of
Michael Manwaring was opened in
1976, specializing in graphic design
and environmental graphics programs.
His work has been the subject of
feature articles in many major periodicals, and he has received numerous awards including gold medals
from the San Francisco Art Directors
Club, the Los Angeles Art Directors
Club, and the New York Art
Directors Club.

Michael Manwaring is the product of two
divergent attitudes. On one hand, he was raised
a Californian, a member of an unconventional
generation in search of new questions and
new answers. On the other hand, he was schooled
in the dogmas of rationalism at the San Francisco
Art Institute during the early 1960s (the
"Swiss Decade" in graphic design). He was
impressed with the typographical philosophies
of **Josef Muller-Brockmann** and other Swiss
masters, admiring their command of spatial
structure, and commitment to pure geometry.
But, despite this, he felt the need to follow his
own path.

Manwaring is a leader of an expressive "California
Style" centered around the San Francisco Bay
area, recognized and imitated throughout
the United States. His intention, however, has
not been to create a new style, but to explore
personal visions and reactions to the complexities
of culture. His work is a record of curious
musings and insightful observations.

In the late sixties, he worked with Gordon
Ashby on the IBM sponsored *Astronomia* exhibition
at the Hayden Planetarium in New York. He
learned from Ashby that "Design is not about
style, nor old versus new. It's about how
one looks at and feels about things." Manwaring
looks at the world differently each time he
views it, remaining faithful to his instincts.

He is an eclectic who finds strange and wonderful
connections between obscure historical references:
"I am more interested in art and architectural
history than design history. Specifically, I

1   Environmental typography for India
    Basin Industrial Park.

2,3   Cover and interior spread from
      a promotional booklet for Kenkay
      Associates, landscape architects.

4   Logotype for Pacific Quadrant
    Development Company.

Michael Manwaring

am fascinated by the **Renaissance**, the Baroque and **Mannerism**—they comprise maybe one-half of my influences. The other half is a combination of nature and contemporary culture. I do like graphic design magazines and books, but they seem to have the lowest priority on my reading table. I also like contemporary poetry because it gives one ideas about imagery and symbols, and also for the way it reads and occupies the page." Manwaring does not seek information and inspiration from obvious sources (such as thumbing through design annuals); he looks for the obscure—life itself—and breaks through the mask of mediocrity, establishing new parameters of design and typography.

With such a synthesis of diverse influences, it is not surprising that Manwaring's work is delicately balanced between order and chaos. He uses an almost obsessive vocabulary of forms. Silhouettes and abstract geometrical motifs, and a wide variety of exotic images and typographic forms are precariously balanced in asymmetrical compositions. The typefaces that he uses are chosen for their visual appeal and appropriateness to the communication, and he often molds typographic forms from line and shape.

Manwaring's poster for a design conference at Stanford University combines type and image into labyrinths of disparate shapes, colors, and textures, revealing a carefully rehearsed, visual pandemonium (Fig. 5). Words occur in a variety of typefaces and sizes, conforming to colored pyramids. "Stanford" is abruptly scrawled through the center of the space, contrasting with the precise geometrical environment and bringing an element of stability to the page. Mysteriously human, silhouettes, positioned with typographical precision, peek from behind green curtains.

Among Manwaring's most notable typographic achievements are his logotypes. His approach is not based on making near-blueprint copies of

6

7

existing abstract corporate logotypes; rather, he uses his distinct lexicon of forms to produce symbols of extraordinary clarity and elegance. For the Robert Finigan Partnership logotype, the letters *R*, *F*, and *P* emerge from a cluster of interdependent and unified lines to denote "partnership" (Fig. 6).

Throughout his career, Manwaring has been involved with a wide range of architectural graphics and exhibition design projects. He is accustomed to working with typography on a large scale. A fine example of this is a three-dimensional sign for the India Basin Industrial Park which features Helvetica letters transformed into an elaborate sculptural configuration (Fig. 1). The appearance of the sign changes throughout the day as light and shadow engage in dialogue.

It is certain that Manwaring's early rationalist training occupies a corner of his mind: "Even though my work may not show it that much, I still think of a page as a problem in geometry. I like to draw an elaborate and complex tissue: lots of lines; discovering relationships and modules; working in two or three different colored pencils; leaving all the construction lines in—it is kind of a game and at the same time a meditation of sorts, not unlike (nor as good as) a Carlo Scrapa drawing."

Manwaring feels his design is successful only if it meets specific criteria: first, it has to solve the client's problem; second, it has to solve the designer's problem (formal and aesthetic); third, it should make a cultural contribution.

He is never satisfied: "My mind and my gut want design to be richer, complex and more symbolic, and I feel that I am heading in that direction. My frustration is that progress is very slow: my skills inadequate to my desire."

8

9

6–8 Logotypes for Robert Finigan Partnership; Eileen West, designers and manufacturers of women's dresses and sleepwear; and Heffalump, a retail store for imported children's toys.

9 Label for the Hanna Winery.

Thomas Ockerse

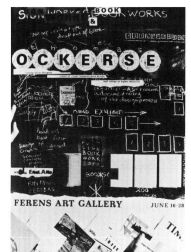

1 Poster for an exhibition of Thomas
Ockerse's work.

2 *26 POEMS? + 1*, a limited-edition
collection of poems.

Only a small number of designers have ventured
beyond safe and familiar practice into unknown
regions of design theory. Those committed
to serious study and documentation of these
puzzles are even fewer. Thomas Ockerse, a
native of Holland, is an exception. His inquiries
have revealed the nature of visual language,
and have perhaps narrowed the gap between
theory and practice. His studio is a virtual
"laboratory" where he performs a wide range of
visual experiments.

A number of experiences contributed to the
shaping of Ockerse's inquisitive mind. He
inherited the Dutch traits of ingenuity, precision,
and discipline. Open-mindedness, another
quality of the Dutch, was a natural part of his
family life. He remembers the theosophic
searchings of his family and their constant quest
for new ideas. Three years before leaving
Holland, Ockerse attended the Kees Boeke
School, one of the most successful experimental
schools in Holland.

It would be difficult to pinpoint exactly when
Ockerse first became interested in design
and typography, but it certainly increased during

2

3

 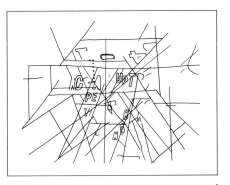

4

his undergraduate and graduate education, and expanded while teaching at Indiana University. While in graduate school in the Yale design program, he sharpened his sensitivity to basic typographic principles. His teachers at this time were **Norman Ives, Herbert Matter,** and **Diter Rot.** The learning was extensive, but Ockerse observes that it was not because these individuals were good "teachers" in the traditional sense. Rather, "They displayed their design wisdom through their mannerisms and their work, and their general attitudes toward working and designing."

Beyond formal education, Ockerse has also scrutinized the philosophies and attitudes of **El Lissitzky, Marcel Duchamp, Piet Zwart, John Cage, Laszlo Moholy-Nagy, Buckminster Fuller,** and **Ian Hamilton Finley,** to name a few. He is careful not to be deceived by historical "facts," believing that, as Napoleon once quipped, "History is a myth that has been agreed upon." Perhaps other humanist fields have influenced him the most: literature, music, philosophy, and theatre.

After leaving graduate school, Ockerse accepted a design position at Indiana University. Here, he became deeply involved with **concrete poetry.** This movement, beginning in the early 1950s with the experiments of **Eugen Gomringer** of Switzerland and the **Noigandres group** of Brazil, reshaped traditional poetry and opened new vistas of exploration in human communication. Words were no longer mere representations of external ideas. Instead, they were perceived as being visual, phonetic, and kinetic—qualities having communicative and expressive possibilities in and of themselves.

5

Thomas Ockerse (born in 1940 in Holland) received his BFA degree in Visual Communication Design at Ohio State University in 1963 and an MFA in Graphic Design from Yale University in 1965. Since 1978 he has been the Head of the Graphic Design Department at the Rhode Island School of Design. In 1965 he established Tom Ockerse Editions (TOE), a private press. He has won many design awards, and he lectures extensively throughout Europe and the United States on the subject of visual language.

3,4   *tvdocumentracings.*

5   **Cover for a limited-edition book of found poetry.**

Thomas Ockerse

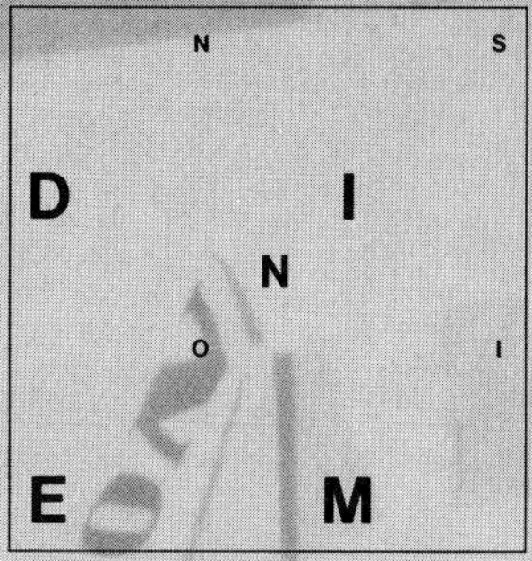

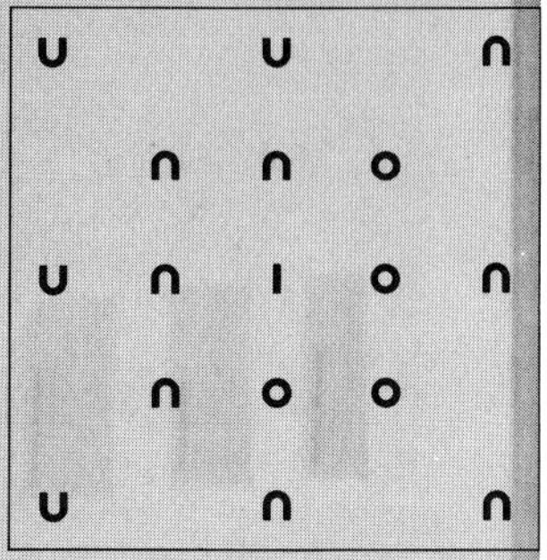

N   S

D   I

N

o

I

E   M

U   U   ∩

∩   ∩   O

U   ∩   I   O   ∩

∩   ∩   O

U   ∩

6

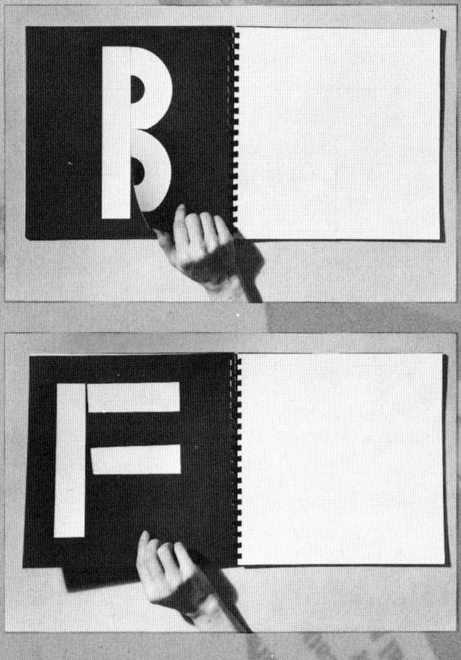

11

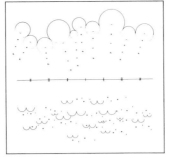

6   Poem, *LOVe/LIVe*.

7–10   Selection of poems from 1969. From left to right are *Dimension*, *UNION*, *Aviation*, *Cloud/Horizon/Water*.

11   The *A–Z Book*.

12   Announcement for Thomas Ockerse Editions (T.O.E.).

An early example of Ockerse's work in this area is the poem *Dimension* (Fig. 7). At first, the poem appears to be a random grouping of letters. But further observation reveals a specific hierarchy. Letters, ranging from large to small, suggest a cube. With this realization, the poem may be read as D-I-M-E / N / S-I-O-N. Perceived in this way, the reader's mind is cued to meaning far beyond that provided by the typical linear format. Through concrete poetry, Ockerse came to fully understand the endless creative possibilities of typography as a dynamic element of visual language. In 1965, Ockerse established TOE (Thomas Ockerse Editions). This private press, in a laboratory setting, has enabled him to apply theory to practice.

Ockerse solves typographic problems in three stages. He first begins with a process called "*de*-signing." This word implies stripping a typographical message to its bare essence, then building a structure based upon functional needs. His goal is to say as much as he can with as few elements as possible.

Secondly, Ockerse responds to the expressive nature of typographic language. "While involved in the creative process, I believe in 'tripping' myself with a sort of Duchampian logic— targeting a result but landing somewhere else." At this stage he pushes beyond convention and preconception. He accomplishes this by "atomizing" the message, a process that determines the meaning of individual parts in relationship to the whole. What emerges is a game-like structure where a reader's mind is taken through a hierarchy of interrelated parts, thereby gaining deeper insight into the message. A participatory book designed by Ockerse demonstrates this concept (Fig. 11). *The A–Z Book* consists of pages with die-cut and printed shapes. As pages are turned, the juxtaposition and interaction of these shapes reveal the twenty-six letters of the alphabet.

In the last step, Ockerse attempts to discover the logical relationships between form, meaning, and function (syntax, semantics, and pragmatics). The tool that he uses to reveal these relationships is **semiotics.** This science studies the nature of signs, the basic elements of language. It was first suggested as a plausible science early in this century with the work of the Swiss linguist, **Ferdinand de Saussure.** The writings of **Charles S. Pierce,** the American founder of semiotics, have perhaps been Ockerse's most significant influence in this area. Ockerse uses semiotics to generate ideas and to evaluate the effectiveness of his solutions. By understanding the nature of visual language with the aid of this instrument, Ockerse is able to objectify tasks, sustain a design strategy, and avoid the problem of becoming deceived in a "tangled web of meaningless form."

12

Jacklin Pinsler

1

atmospheric grays and crisp drawing create
a palpable sense of weather, time and place.

Edgar Degas has always been considered
one of the greatest of the French Impressionists
and is known for his inclusion of tense psycho-
logical moments, as well as the spontaneity, light
and color that characterize the style generally.
He was greatly interested in interior scenes,
especially those of dancers in rehearsal or performance. In Ballerina, Russian Dancer (fig. 22),
the performer and the anonymous spectator are
linked by the glowing color that unifies the space,
while generating a sense of the excitement of
the theater.

Maurice de Vlaminck's Landscape (fig. 23)
manifests the bold colors characteristic of the
late painting of Cézanne. But marking the painting even more strongly are the sculptural planes
similar to those that Picasso and Braque carved
out of the landscape in their early Cubist paintings. Much like the Vlaminck, but even more
sculptured and stylized, is the Landscape with
Gardener (fig. 20) by André L'Hote. A late Cubist,

19

Sorel Etrog | Sunbird | 1967 | 90 inches high
Located at Electrolux, Bristol, Virginia

Continued on page 28 ▶

24

1 Interior page from a catalog on
   the Nathan Cummings art collection.

2 Packaging typography for Casa
   De Vida.

Jacklin Pinsler arrived in Chicago from Hertzelia, Israel at age twelve totally unfamiliar with the English language. She first learned to recognize roman letterforms through street signs, graffiti, magazines, and other forms of pedestrian typography. These early impressions were the unconscious seeds of a lifelong fascination with typography.

Years later, at the University of Illinois, Pinsler pursued serious study in design. **David Colley,** her most influential teacher at the time, helped her to understand the intricate nature of typographic language, its visual syntax and grammar, and its ability to enhance and intensify meaning. She grasped the nuances of this language, and in the process, discovered it to be only one part of a much larger, universal language of form applicable to many areas of artistic endeavor.

"As a point of reference," Pinsler remarks, "I make use of other fields of artistic expression— from dance to photography, as well as architecture, painting, and sculpture." The **Prouns** of **El Lissitzky,** the stencilled words and numbers of **Jasper Johns,** and the **photoplastics** of **Laszlo Moholy-Nagy** have each found their way into Pinsler's work. She has also been guided by the formative ideas of **Constructivism** and **de Stijl.** This is not to imply that she proceeds blindly as an imitator of styles, or that her work is blatantly historicist. On the contrary, her preoccupation is with ideas and provocative communication, not with stylistic embellishment.

After leaving school, Pinsler searched for a job that would provide her with a wide variety of experiences in visual problem solving. Collaboration with Diane Kavalarus at *Cuisine* magazine infused her work with discipline and provided her with an eye for typographic refinement. At Crosby Associates, Inc. (a firm widely known for the design of corporate communications) Pinsler perfected an expressive, yet functional, style. While her approach is in line with the Chicago corporate tradition, it is neither rigid nor dogmatic. She has softened its edges: "My work has evolved aesthetically from a controlled, uncomplicated translation to

2

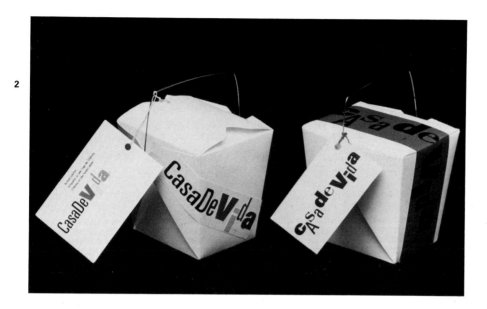

Jacklin Pinsler (born in 1953 in Hertzelia, Israel) is Design Director at Crosby Associates, Inc., in Chicago, involved primarily in corporate identity and financial communications. She was educated at the University of Illinois, receiving her BFA in Graphic Design in 1976. Her work has been honored with awards from the American Institute of Graphic Arts, the Society of Typographic Arts, and the New York Art Directors Club; and it has appeared in major design publications, including *Novum Gebrauchsgraphik*, *Industrial Design* magazine, and *Art Direction* magazine.

3

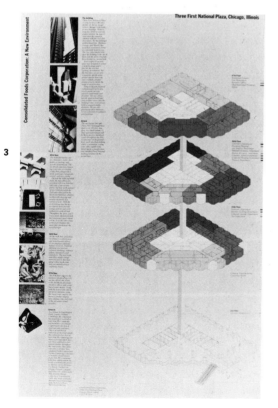

4

NUVEEN

3   Poster for Consolidated Foods Corporation.

4   Logotype for John Nuveen & Co. Inc., investment bankers.

Jacklin Pinsler

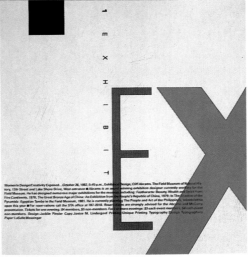

a more abstract, expressive, and emotional interpretation. Through use of juxtaposition, fragmentation, and tension I manipulate the physical letterforms to evoke an appropriate feeling."

Pinsler enlivens the typographic page by balancing her work between structure and control, vigor and freedom. These dichotomies are aptly illustrated by a series of announcements designed for the organization Women in Design (Figs. 6–9). Brightly colored compositions, splashed with an array of letters, shapes, and textures, appear mildly schizophrenic; yet, they possess a sense of order. Structure is derived from a single, prominent letterform serving as an armature upon which all other elements within the composition are built. Pinsler "constructs" her compositions, bringing unity to diversity.

Typographic manipulations are used by Pinsler to separate, connect, and emphasize the elements of a page. These transform space into stimulating visual environments while also establishing clarity and legibility. For example, an art exhibition catalog based upon a two-column grid features generously leaded Futura Bold text type (Fig. 1). Sprinkled throughout the text are titles of paintings underlined with a delicate rule and accentuated with slightly larger, bold initial caps. This text type glistens

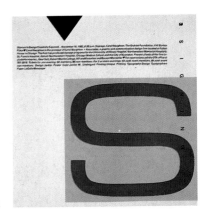

5   **Letterhead for Arnold Zann Photography.**

6–9   **Announcements for a series of events sponsored by** *Women in Design*.

and enables a reader to immediately connect titles of paintings to respective illustrations. The pages of the catalog are further punctuated by thin vertical rules used to separate text from illustrations, to distinguish specific facts within captions, and to highlight folios.

Pinsler's experimentations enable her to reveal memorable visual analogies. In a letterhead design for Arnold Zann Photography, an imposing letter *A*, in sunburst yellow, appears out of focus (Fig. 5). Its soft, irresolute quality contrasts with a crisp, geometrical letter *Z*, rigidly anchored to the upper left-hand corner of the page, establishing a structural framework. The engaging dialogue between these two letters suggests a photographic theme and provides unexpected typographic contrast. The analogy is carried further with the letters "A–Z" signifying completeness.

Because Pinsler feels that "people are immune to what is expected," she manipulates visual language through a process of "visual improvisation." "The most valuable thing I have learned," she explains, "is to be open to changes at any given point in the design process."

9

Women In Design/Creativity Exposed...November 17, 1982, 5:30 p.m., Reception and forum featuring Cliff Abrams, Margaret I. McCurry, and Carol Naughton, The Graham Foundation, 4 W. Burton Place. A. Robin Orden, moderator ■ Concluding the series, a panel discussion and open forum moderated by A. Robin Orden, promises to be a stimulating event bringing together elements of the individual presentations with an overview of how each discipline reflects the creative process in general. Emphasis will be placed on issues of interest to the audience with ample opportunity for questions ▼ Orden was a founding member and first co-president of Women In Design/N.Y. She is currently a consultant/facilitator working with design organizations on a national design network ● Refreshments will be served. For reservations call the STA office at 787-2018. Tickets for one evening: $4 members, $5 non-members. For 2 or more evenings: $3 each event members, $4 each event non-members. Design:Jacklin Pinsler Copy:Janice M. Lindergard Printing:Unique Printing Typography:Design Typographers Paper:LaSalle Messinger

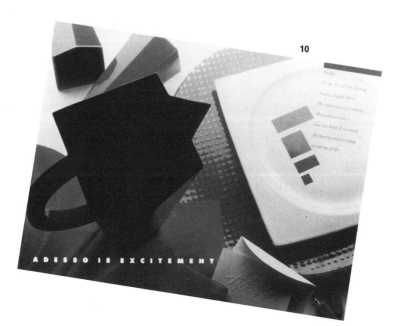

10

10 Catalog cover for Adesso, manufacturer of ceramics.

Woody Pirtle

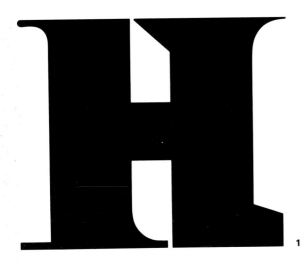

1

At a very early age Woody Pirtle was destined for a life as a graphic designer. "When I was a child," he recalls, "our family travelled a great deal. As far back as I can remember, I have been enamored with road signs and chiselled letters on historic buildings. My gravitation towards this field was a natural one resulting from my curiosity about typography." Now Pirtle is one of the best-known designers in America—a prodigy of the Lone Star state.

He began his formal education at the University of Arkansas where he briefly studied architecture. Not satisfied with this direction, he found himself in the fine arts, eventually earning a degree. He had never received specific training in graphic design, and until he met Stan Richards of the Richards Group, he relied exclusively upon his own observations. Like several other up-and-coming young designers working in Dallas during the early 1970s, Pirtle was hired and groomed by Richards in a transplanted New York style of design. This style was both expressive and diverse, and possessed a touch of sophisticated humor. Pirtle felt comfortable with this pluralistic attitude towards visual problem solving, and he absorbed it into his work.

2

1   Logotype for Robert J. Hilton Co.,
Inc., Typographers.

2   Interior spread from
an annual report for National
Gypsum Company.

3

In his search for understanding and inspiration, Pirtle became aware of the value of design history as a reference point for his work. It led him away from gimmicks and graphic sleights of hand; and out of respect for the remarkable designers of the past, it led him to a design approach of quality and integrity. He found legibility and beauty to be of equal importance. **Frederic Goudy, A. M. Cassandre, Herb Lubalin, Paul Rand,** and **Tom Carnase** are those who have most significantly influenced Pirtle's work over the years.

Early in his development, Pirtle produced a high volume of custom-made letterforms, Spencerian scripts and calligraphy (perhaps prompted by Carnase's influence); and while he still enjoys working with elegant letterforms, he does not have the time to do so. His design methodology has evolved into one that is spontaneous and deceptively simple. Ideas bubble just beneath the surface as he makes mental jottings of design possibilities. Then, Pirtle says, "as I begin to dissect a problem, the solution always seems to emerge—sometimes as though it were staring me in the face." Solutions are never predetermined; they evolve in response to the specific nature of each situation. The spontaneity of Pirtle's thought processes enables him to cover all bases without bogging down under the weight of meaningless trivia. Brevity and simplicity are his overriding concerns.

4

5

Woody Pirtle (born in 1943 in Corsicana, Texas) is President and Creative Director of Pirtle Design, Inc., a multifaceted design firm. He graduated from the University of Arkansas with a BFA degree in Art in 1967. His work has received wide acclaim throughout the international design community via exhibitions, periodicals, and books. Major profiles about his work are presented in *Seven Graphic Designers, The Business of Graphic Design,* and *100 Texas Posters.* He is a member of the Alliance Graphique Internationale, and was elected to the board of directors of the American Institute of Graphic Arts in 1982.

3–5 Logotypes for Ansel Art Center (unpublished); Landa Pharmaceutical; Mr. and Mrs. Aubrey Hair.

Woody Pirtle

6

Humor and surprise are often achieved through the use of unusual visual metaphors. By this means, viewers are lulled into Pirtle's perceptual fantasies, unable to take his visual messages for granted. Outstanding examples include a logotype for an art supply store that is simultaneously read as a splatter of ink and the letter A; and a mark for a pharmaceutical company that functions both as an open capsule and the letter L (Figs. 3,4). Whether he is loosely sketching on napkins, cutting and tearing shapes for collages, constructing precise geometrical diagrams, or solving problems with computer-generated photomontages, the same whimsical flair prevails. While Pirtle is willing to stick his neck out for an inventive solution, his bottom line is to solve problems for clients.

It is apparent in Pirtle's work that type and image are inseparable; together, they function as integral components of a message. A poster for the opening of the *Tango* nightclub in Dallas features letterforms and vibrant images dancing to the same frantic rhythms (Fig. 6). The relationship is further strengthened by the use of letterforms with sharp serifs echoing the razor-edged dancers. In another example—an architectural poster—type and image are wedded through contrast (Fig. 8). Loosely scrawled handwriting accentuates the geometrical precision and harmony of architectural forms. Correspondence between these elements is also attained through similarity in size and in spatial placement. In each of these examples, type and image are carefully joined for maximum effect. Pirtle's attention to typographic detail and impeccable craftsmanship enhance the clarity and aesthetic quality of his visual communication.

"Inventive ideas," says Pirtle, "are the backbone of our business, and the best work I produce presents a message in the most direct, streamlined fashion. I'm not interested in graphic trends, or even in a recognizable style—I'm proudest of work that is graphically compelling, crystal clear as a communications vehicle and stylistically timeless."

7

8

9

STUDIOS

10

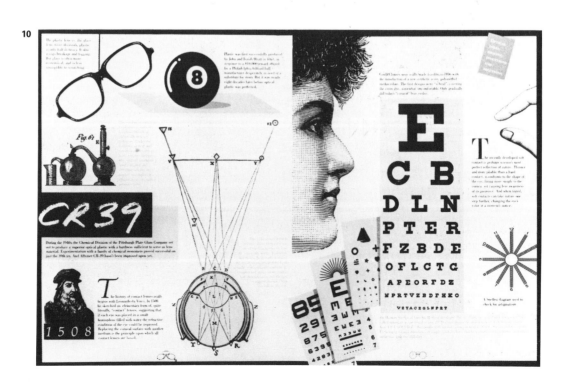

Paul Rand

1

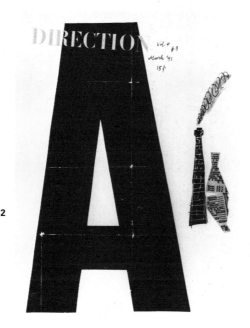

2

Paul Rand has lived the life of a legend for nearly half a century. Brilliant, contemptuous, intense, critical, and eloquent, he has over his long career become a guru of design and a guardian of visual principles. He is perhaps the most revered, envied, and respected of America's graphic designers.

Rand studied art and design at Pratt Institute, Parsons School of Design, the Brooklyn Institute of Arts and Sciences, and with George Grosz at the Art Students League. George Switzer, an early industrial designer, helped Rand to be aware of the new design expressions trickling out of Europe at the time.

Rand began his career at the youthful age of twenty-three as the art director of *Esquire* and *Apparel Arts* magazines. At the time, graphic communication was dominated by homey illustrations, headlines, and text placed in uneventful, symmetrical compositions. Rand, informed by the modern art movements in Europe during the 1920s, had a very different conception of form and space. In *Paul Rand: A Designer's Art*, he discusses the impact of modernism: "The revolution in modern painting, with its emphasis on form, on abstraction, on visual relationships, on unorthodox methods and materials, has played its part in focusing attention on the design of the total surface rather than on anecdote or subject matter."

From the writings and work of such visionaries as Cezanne, **Picasso, Kandinsky,** and Klee, Rand discovered the expressive potential of color, texture, collage, montage, gesture, and visual contrast. Circles, squares, rectangles, dots, triangles, gestural signs, and other elemental shapes are used abundantly in his work; indeed, they have become his trademark. These elements, which he brings into a dynamic spatial equilibrium, appear in a wide variety of media.

1,2 Magazine covers for *Direction*.

3

4

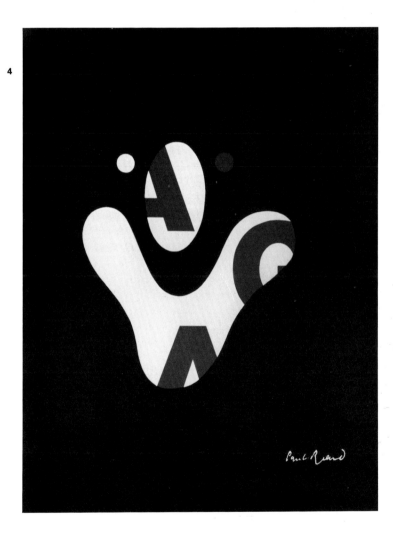

Paul Rand (born in 1914 in New York City) has been a design consultant to major American corporations since 1956. These include IBM, Cummins Engine Company, and Westinghouse Electric. Also since 1956 he has taught at Yale University, where he is now Professor Emeritus of Graphic Design. Among his awards are: Doctor of Fine Arts (Honorary) from the Philadelphia College of Art and the Parsons School of Design, the Hall of Fame of the New York Art Directors Club, the Gold Medal of the American Institute of Graphic Arts, and the Medal of the Type Directors Club.

3　Advertisement for Westinghouse Electric Corporation.

4　Cover design for the American Institute of Graphic Arts.

Paul Rand

Paracelsus

Selected Writings

Second Edition, Revised

Edited by Jolande Jacobi
Bollingen Series XXVIII
Pantheon Books

---

5   Book jacket for *Paracelsus*.

---

6   Logotype for IBM.

This experimental use of form not only makes it possible for Rand to elevate advertising design to the status of art and satisfy his urge for creative expression; it also enables him to create symbols through the interrelationships and inherent qualities of form. "It is in symbolic, visual terms that the designer ultimately realizes his perceptions and experiences; and it is in a world of symbols that man lives. The symbol is thus the common language between artist and spectator."

Rand establishes the essence of subject matter through the use of powerful elemental and pictographic signs. He believes that symbols are capable of representing many different ideas through juxtaposition, association, and analogy: "The circle as opposed to the square, for instance, as a pure form evokes a specific aesthetic sensation; ideologically, it is the sign of eternity, without beginning or end. A red circle may be interpreted as the sign of the sun, the Japanese flag, a stop sign, an ice-skating rink, or a special brand of coffee . . . *depending on its context*." In a cover for the **American Institute of Graphic Arts,** for example, Rand combines letters and a rebus (an eye substituted for the letter *I*) within a circle to signify a mask (Fig. 8).

Rand also employs letterforms as symbolic form. He observes that "A single letter says more than a thousand words. . . . The dual reading is what makes such images memorable.

7

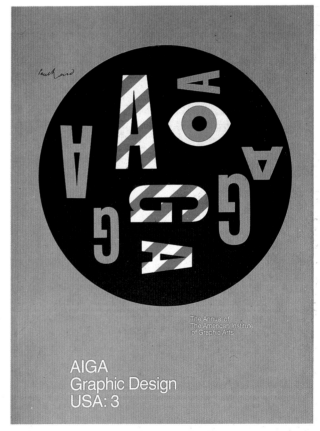

They amuse as they inform." Rand's effective Westinghouse logo, which is composed of simple geometrical shapes, simultaneously suggests wires and plugs, electronic circuitry, and the letter "W" (Fig. 3).

However, Rand does not always attempt to symbolize the subject matter by the visual character of images. He often uses mnemonic devices (graphic elements such as stripes, circles, and contrasting forms that help viewers to remember images). Stripes, for example, is the mnemonic device used to create the IBM logotype (Fig. 6). While stripes have no direct relationship to computers, they have come to symbolize them because of their use in the IBM logotype. Another example of Rand's use of mnemonic devices is the NeXT logotype (Fig. 7). Here, three factors exist that make this a memorable mark: the lowercase *e* combined with three uppercase letters to establish contrast, the use of a black cube, and the word *NeXT* split into two lines. Breaking words in this way has become familiar over the years with examples such as **Robert Indiana's** *LOVE* sculpture.

In his design process, Rand combines both intellectual and intuitive problem-solving skills. He believes that more must be done than randomly pushing things around on a page: "The experienced designer does not begin with some preconceived idea. Rather, the idea is (or should be) the result of careful observation, and the design a product of that idea . . . the designer experiences, perceives, analyzes, organizes, symbolizes, synthesizes."

These steps, whether consciously applied or not, are essential for responsible design practice, and for the essential integration of form and function. Rand declares: "Visual communications of any kind, whether persuasive or informative, from billboards to birth announcements, should be seen as the embodiment of form and function: the integration of the beautiful and the useful. Copy, art, and typography should be seen as a living entity; each element integrally related, in harmony with the whole, and essential to the execution of an idea."

7   **Symbol for NeXT, a computer company.**

8   **Cover design for the American Institute of Graphic Arts.**

Paula Scher

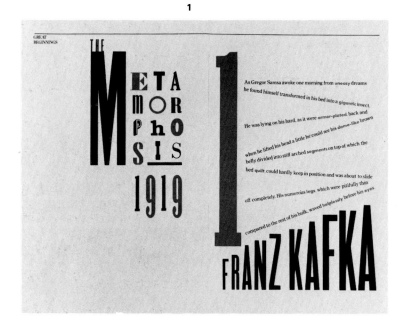

1

2

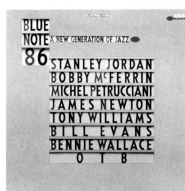

3

1   Spread from *Great Beginnings*, a
     promotional booklet for Koppel
     and Scher and celebration of great
     literary beginnings.

2   Album cover for *Gidon Kremer,
     Romantic Miniatures for Violin,*
     CBS Records.

3   Album cover for Blue Note Records.

In 1968, when Paula Scher was a graphic
design student at the Tyler School of Art, she
was afraid of typography. It was the weak
link in her development. She was interested in
ideas and images. "I really wanted to be an
illustrator," she admits, "except I discovered that
I couldn't draw." Out of necessity she moved
to New York in 1970, became a graphic
designer, and began to explore typographic
possibilities. She became passionate about type
in 1974 while designing record covers. The
record industry ran out of money in 1979, a
calamity that forced Scher to cut costs by
creating covers restricted to typography. This
unfortunate situation at CBS Records was a
blessing for Scher, for she could take advantage
of her unlimited curiosity, examine the roots
of typography, its innumerable applications,
and launch her prodigious typographic vision.

Stanislaw Zagorski, Scher's design and illustration
teacher for three years, nurtured her visual
thinking abilities. The most significant and
lasting influence has been **Seymour Chwast,** who
taught her where to look: "My love of the
Victoriana, Art Nouveau and **Art Deco** came
from him . . . Seymour taught me design as a
way of life."

Over the years, Scher has developed a profound
respect for early twentieth-century design.
Her inquiring mind pursues sources that inspire
and imbue her work with visual richness and
diversity, and she freely expresses this fact:
"I owe everything to historical references. I love
all periods (of design) until 1950." Such
pivotal figures as **El Lissitzky, Alexander Rodchenko, Kasimir Malevich, Filippo Marinetti,
Laszlo Moholy-Nagy, Herbert Bayer, W. A.
Dwiggins,** and **A. M. Cassandre** have influenced
her from time to time. A single work will
often allude to several of these influences
at once. At other times Scher will pay homage
to one specific individual or style. Two examples are a promotional poster designed by Scher
for Columbia Records that uses tightly clustered,
sans serif type of various sizes and weights
in an angular structure reminiscent of Russian
Constructivism (Fig. 10), and a poster design
for the School of Visual Arts that integrates

broad, simplified planes of color with type, strongly suggesting the work of Cassandre (Fig. 8). These designs go far beyond superficial mimicry of past styles. Scher extends typographic precedents and tradition with clarity and wit.

Humor is used often in Scher's work. In a poster for Swatch, Scher shapes a visual/verbal pun around **Herbert Matter's** masterful Swiss travel poster of 1934 (Fig. 9). A large idealized image of a smiling woman in the original poster (see Page 137 in Major Resources) is replaced with her contemporary counterpart, who is extending a watch-clad arm diagonally through the composition. The two watches on the woman's wrist replace a Swiss cross, and the word *Schwiez* is substituted with a screaming red *Swatch*. This is a humorous metaphor when viewed by a discerning designer, but the general audience probably misses the point.

Scher relies upon typefaces from past periods and styles when making selections. She tries to use type that will accurately convey an idea, and complement or contrast a photograph or illustration. A promotional project for Champion entitled *Beautiful Faces* illustrates this point (Figs. 4–6). It presents a selection of eccentric and decorative typefaces selected from a variety of sources—from old type books discovered in antique shops to specimens found at the Smithsonian Institution. Scher created several designs, each composed of two typefaces from the collection. These designs are based upon the visual characteristics of the letterforms, the compatibility of each pair, and a broad range of styles and periods.

4

5

6

Paula Scher (born in 1948 in Washington, D.C.) was raised in Virginia and Maryland. She received her BFA degree from the Tyler School of Art in 1970. After being in the record industry for several years, she opened the New York based design office, Koppel and Scher. Her numerous awards include Gold Medals from the Art Directors Club of New York and the Society of Illustrators, four Grammy nominations from the National Association for Recording Arts and Sciences, and she was named one of Ten Significant Women Designers in America by Women in Design, Chicago.

4–6 Promotion for Champion's Color Collection. This is an eclectic collection of eccentric and decorative type and typographic designs illustrating their use.

Paula Scher

7

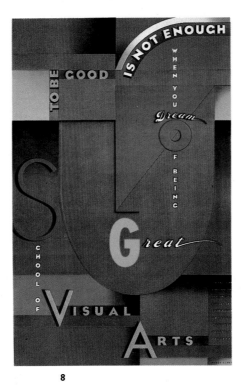

8

9

An eclectic approach to problem solving is in itself the unifying feature of Scher's work, for ultimately a montage of possibilities enables her to place equal emphasis on form and content. The visual style associated with Scher's work is the embodiment of a vocabulary derived from many historical sources. She does not follow a set of rigid formal typographic rules limiting a free and spontaneous approach; rather, she intuitively defines the limitations of each problem as it unfolds. Indeed, Scher is suspicious of any design formula or dogma.

As one dedicated to quality, Scher is very concerned about the present-day corruption of original typeface designs. She detests bastardizations of authentic typefaces. "I am greatly concerned about the disappearance of original cuts of typefaces. I think ITC is responsible for some of this, and the crude digitization of classic faces like Bodoni Book is just as bad." Scher is skeptical of new technology, for she fears that designers will rely too heavily on machinery as opposed to their own creativity. She puts things in proper perspective: "Equipment is equipment, and art is art . . . If an artist uses a computer instead of an exacto-knife he still has to be an artist . . . I personally don't like computers and prefer the knife."

Scher has an endless appetite for design and approaches her work with vigorous energy: "I am a graphic professional. My first goal is to communicate. Sometimes I need to be quiet and sometimes I need to scream. I am always making an impression. I want to create work that startles, surprises, and amuses. I never enjoy doing anything neutral, nor do I do it well. Typography is one vehicle that I use, but it is only one. I don't enjoy doing stylistic approaches purely for their own sake. I use them to make a point, to complement an idea, to create nostalgia or a specific ambiance. I'm always looking for a reason to do things. What gives me the most pleasure are those pieces of work that contain a strong idea and an equally strong design. But design must also serve the idea. I'm happiest when the work is witty. If the audience doesn't appreciate the design — maybe I'll succeed in making them smile."

10

R. D. Scudellari

ROBERT GRAVES

I, CLAUDIUS

MODERN LIBRARY

1

Long after most graphic ephemera has been crumpled and hauled off with the trash, books remain forever to instruct, to inspire, to entertain. Robert Scudellari has devoted his entire career to the design and art direction of books worthy of their purpose.

Scudellari's interest in books was ignited by **George Salter,** a teacher at Cooper Union who taught calligraphy, book design, and illustration. Salter became well-known for literally hundreds of extraordinary book jackets designed for several publishers, Alfred A. Knopf being the most notable. "The Salter Book Aesthetic" became a feature of Random House, Inc., which includes Knopf.

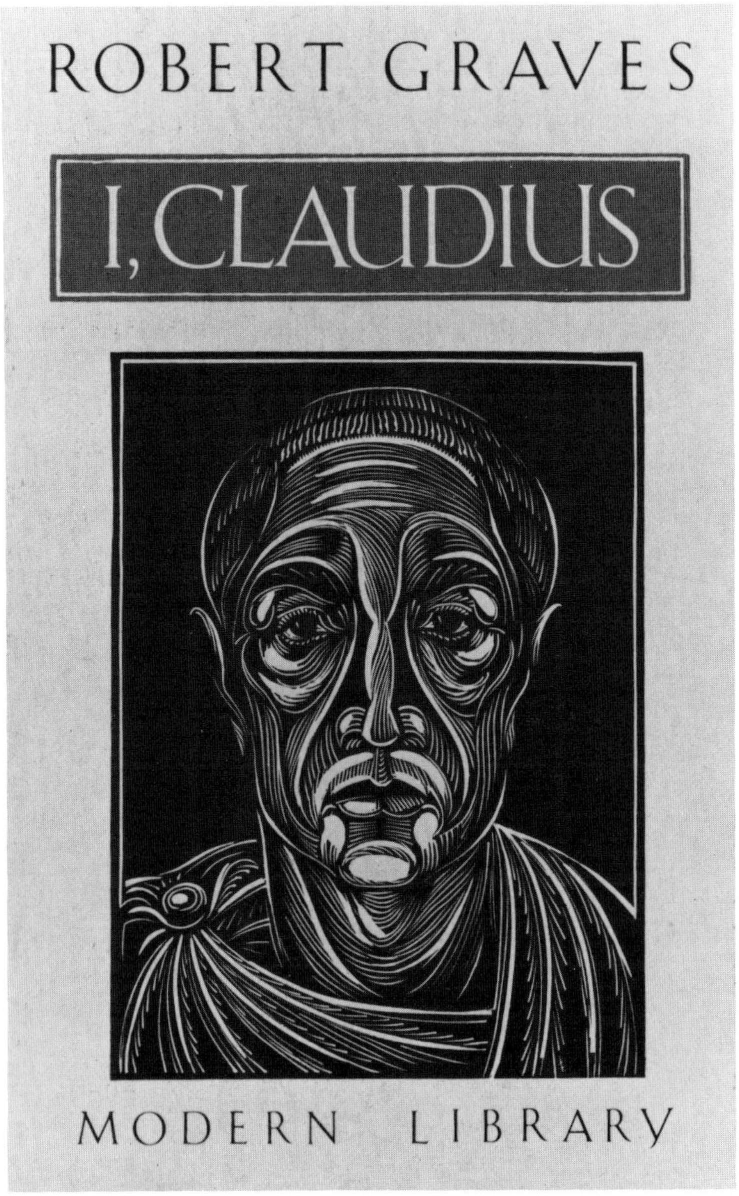

In 1965, Scudellari became Vice President of Graphics at Random House, Inc. He directs the firm's corporate graphics and supervises the design departments of the company's separate publishing divisions. These include Random House, Alfred A. Knopf, Pantheon, Vintage Books, and Modern Library. Each of these publishing houses maintains strict autonomy within the corporate structure; each manages its own list, and each is responsible for both editorial and graphic design decisions.

These publishing houses have developed individual styles that have evolved very slowly over the years. Knopf books, for example, employ a "Dwiggins type of ornamentation," while Random House books are bold, simple, and direct. Pantheon books are extremely eclectic (refer to profile on Louise Fili, page 40). These styles, however, are loosely defined, for while the art directors are aware of stylistic tendencies, it is understood that the nature of each book dictates the design solution. Style never overpowers appropriateness. Scudellari coordinates, offers advice, and resolves conflicts when needed, but he adamantly refuses to meddle in graphic design decisions. He feels that the most valued resource at Random House is talented people; to disrupt their creative flow would be counterproductive.

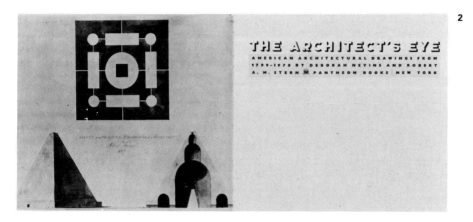

R. D. Scudellari (born in 1933 in New York City) was educated at Cooper Union. For twenty years he has served as Vice President of Graphic Arts at Random House, Inc. Previously he was designer/art director at Harper and Row, Western Printing, and Dell Publishing. He participates in the National Endowment for the Arts program of evaluating government graphics and is a former Vice President of the American Institute of Graphic Arts. His work frequently wins national and international awards.

Standards of design quality remain high within each of the publishing divisions, and this is due in part to the acquisition of Alfred A. Knopf in 1960. Mr. Knopf stressed the design aspects of books as much as content—a revolutionary approach to publishing in the 1920s. He thought books should be endowed with a soul, should be prized for their physical appearance, as works of art. Under the Borzoi imprint, Knopf hired only the best of designers to carry the torch—**W. A. Dwiggins, Warren Chappell,** George Salter, **Paul Rand,** and **Alvin Lustig,** among them.

When Donald Klopfer and Bennett Cerf founded Random House in 1927, they also were aware of the need for excellence in design and typog-

1   Book jacket for *I, Claudius*. Woodcut illustration and co-design by Steven Alcorn.

2   Title spread for *The Architect's Eye*. Drawing by Michael Graves.

3   Interior spread for *Architecture*. Photograph by Richard Payne.

R. D. Scudellari

4 Interior spread for *The World of Rockwell Kent.* Wood engravings by Rockwell Kent.

5 Book jacket for *Children of Light.*

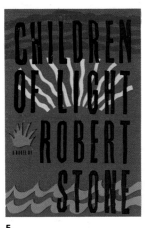

5

raphy. This concern led them to commission **Rockwell Kent** as designer and illustrator of their first title. This was Voltaire's *Candide*, a stunning book that, according to Scudellari "is no less contemporary today than in 1928." This book seems to have influenced Scudellari significantly, for it helped him to understand that books are "timeless," and based upon the universal typographic principles of legibility, readability, and beauty. "The book designer's craft is based upon classic typographic knowledge . . . the book experience, and therefore the book designer's aesthetic, has remained faithful to the classic book qualities for centuries."

In addition to supervising the art departments of the various publishing divisions, Scudellari works on selected projects from among all of the imprints. He is tuned to the visual idiosyncrasies of each, but does not allow this knowledge to smother his personal aesthetic vision. Nor does he allow contemporary trends to dominate his approach: "American typography is ever-changing, as are all of the visual professions. A personal typographic viewpoint is naturally affected by trends, however, it is essential that a designer's visual aesthetic manifest itself regardless of the subjective period of typography."

Scudellari's book jackets are poster-like. They present succinct visual messages often dominated by expressive letterforms—phototype, hand-drawn letters, stencilled letters, distorted letters, calligraphy, etc.—denoting a book's content and engaging a reader's imagination. A jacket for John Le Carre's *The Little Drummer Girl* marches to the staccato rhythms of angular type accented with cadenced lines (Fig. 7). When images or photographs are used, they serve to round-out or complete a message. In a jacket for the *New York City Ballet*, Scudellari uses overlapping outline type to frame and duplicate the qualities of a delicate, statuesque image of dancers (Fig. 6).

A book interior design for *The World Of Rockwell Kent* is a celebration of classical typography and a study in elegant contrasts (Fig. 4). "Venetian blind" blocks of Kennerly type and vivid illustrations by Rockwell Kent are placed within generous margins. The interplay of light and dark, texture and tone, provide the pages with a startling brilliance. This design is not old or new; it is suspended in time. Twenty, fifty, maybe hundreds of years from now, it will retain its value as an aesthetic carrier of information. "The life of a good book," trusts Scudellari, "is timeless."

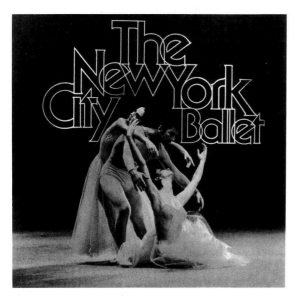

6

7

8

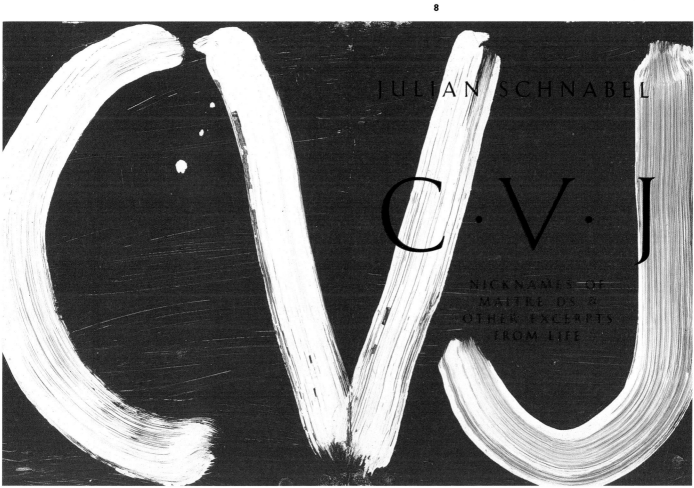

Bradbury Thompson

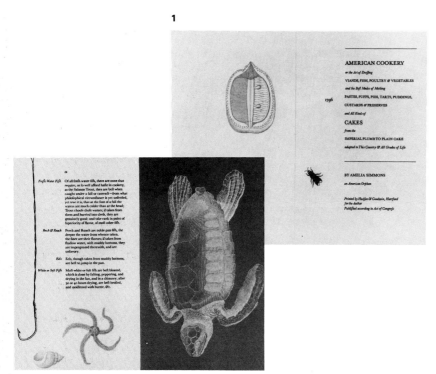

1

2

"Type can be a tool, a toy, and a teacher; it can provide a means of livelihood, a hobby for relaxation, an intellectual stimulant—and a spiritual satisfaction. I believe an avid interest in Type necessarily includes a zest for everyday life." These words, written by Bradbury Thompson in 1956, are what he has lived by during a career spanning fifty years.

Thompson was born, raised, and schooled in Topeka, Kansas. He has many fond memories of his early heartland experiences, particularly of the people who contributed to his earliest development as a designer: his family and teachers (especially his high school journalism teacher and college track coach). He attended Washburn College, where he served as the editor and designer of the school's publication, and although his major was economics, his work on this publication signaled the beginning of a brilliant career in publication design. While in college he also developed discipline by working as a draftsman for roads and bridges.

In 1938, Thompson was off to New York where on his first job he was asked to design an issue of *Westvaco Inspirations*. Over the next twenty-two years he edited and designed sixty issues of this publication. In a way, *Westvaco Inspirations* was Thompson's personal

1,2 Two spreads from *American Cookery* by Amelia Simmons, Westvaco Library of American Classics.

3 Interior spread from *Westvaco Inspirations*.

3

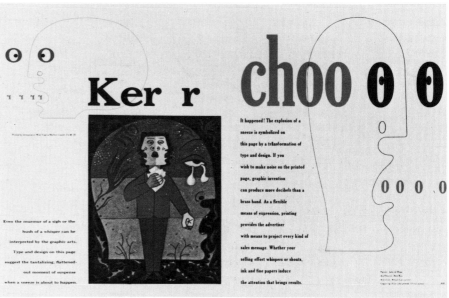

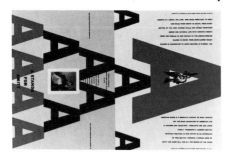
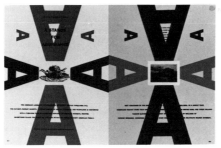

typographic journal. Issue after dazzling issue presented the audience with his ideas, demonstrating that visuals could carry as much — if not more — information as verbal content.

Westvaco provided Thompson with almost unlimited resources for four-color printing, paper, and typography; but there was virtually no budget for illustrative material. He borrowed engravings, photographs, and artwork from advertising agencies, museums, and magazines. His collection of old encyclopedias was another source of visual material. Thompson reflects: "I often found myself digging through the archives of old engravings for illustrations and I became one of the best scroungers in my profession. In designing *Westvaco Inspirations*, the printing press, the typecase, and the print shop were my canvas, my easel, and my second studio." These restrictions became strengths rather than weaknesses, and served to stimulate a dynamic and tactile creative process.

Letters and shapes functioned as expressive symbols to enhance traditional images, and to imply specific meaning. A witty example is found in a 1949 issue. Thompson transformed type into a sneeze both seen and "heard" by the viewer (Fig. 3). Letterforms are cleverly repeated to create the illusion of a nasal explosion. He also experimented with the abstract nature of letterforms, and the subtle shades of meaning derived from simple syntactic manipulations. In an issue dedicated to exploring each of the letters in the word *AMERICA*, for example, the letter *A* is presented in two ways: on its side as an asymmetrical form in motion; and in a mirror-like symmetrical pose of stability and strength (Figs. 4,5).

The pure process colors of magenta, cyan, yellow, and black are those most familiar in Thompson's prismatic work. He often employs them with type and overlapping images of static line engravings to suggest motion and vibration.

6

Bradbury Thompson (born in 1911 in Topeka, Kansas) has served as a design consultant to several important organizations over the years. These include Westvaco Corporation, McGraw-Hill Publications, Time-Life Books, Harvard University, and the Oxford University Press. Also since 1956 he has been a Senior Critic and Visiting Professor at the Yale School of Art. His many significant honors include the Gold Medal of the American Institute of Graphic Arts, Hall of Fame of the New York Art Directors Club, Herb Lubalin Award of the Society of Publication Designers, and the Medal of the Type Directors Club.

4,5   Two spreads from *Westvaco Inspirations 192.*

6   Page from a 1945 edition of *Westvaco Inspirations*. This page discusses and illustrates Bradbury Thompson's Monalphabet.

9

America's
A B C
Libraries
X Y Z
USA 20c
Legacies To Mankind

Bradbury Thompson

7

Thompson is an advocate of clear communication and functional typography. He developed theories about typographic reform, many of which were presented in *Westvaco Inspirations*. In 1945, he created the Monalphabet, using lowercase forms for both large and small letters. He found that the use of two different symbols for the same sound (upper and lowercase) was inefficient and confusing—particularly to children learning to read. Five years later, he developed Alphabet 26, a system using only one symbol for each of the letters of the alphabet. (These experiments are similar to those of **Herbert Bayer,** who invented a "universal alphabet" in 1925.)

In addition to working on *Westvaco Inspirations*, Thompson also served as the art director and designer of *Mademoiselle* and *Art News*. During his career, he designed the formats of nearly three dozen publications, including the prestigious *Smithsonian* magazine, which still uses his original design.

Books have been a crucial part of his career. Of special note are his designs for Westvaco's Library of American Classics, a series of stunning limited-edition books produced to demonstrate the performance of the company's paper. In designing these special editions, Thompson conveyed a sense of the modern world while also preserving the flavor of the times in which the books were originally published.

This is a concern also demonstrated in his design of the *Washburn College Bible*. Completed in 1979, this book is the pinnacle of Thompson's espousal of the flush-left, ragged-right style of typesetting (Fig. 8). It is set in single columns of Sabon Antiqua, a typeface designed by **Jan Tschichold** and based upon the 1540 designs of Claude Garamond. The lines are broken into individual phrases according to the cadence of speech, making reading easier and

7   Page from *Westvaco Inspirations 210*.

8   Interior spread from the *Washburn College Bible*.

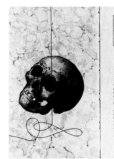

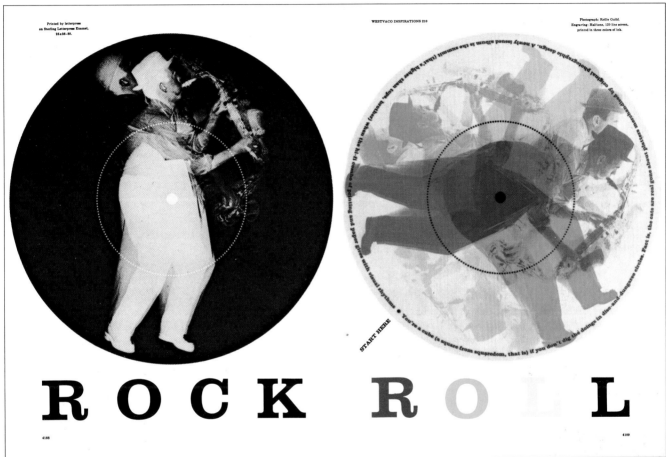

Printed by letterpress
on Sterling Letterpress Enamel,
25 x 38 - 80.

WESTVACO INSPIRATIONS 210

Photograph: Rollie Guild.
Engraving: Halftone, 120 line screen,
printed in three colors of ink.

START HERE

ROCK ROLL

4188

4189

meaning clearer. Thompson's expertise is
not restricted to publications. He has designed
a number of trademarks, and over eighty
stamps for the United States Postal Service.

Keeping typographic traditions alive by absorbing
them into modern themes is perhaps Thompson's most significant contribution, and whether
he is composing visual lullabies or dramatic
marches, his graphic exuberance prevails.

9   Stamp design for the United States
     Postal Service.

10,11   Two spreads from *Tales* by Edgar
         Allan Poe, Westvaco Library of
         American Classics.

12   Interior spread from *Westvaco
      Inspirations 210.*

Massimo Vignelli

In the 1950s a universal attitude calling for a total approach to design emanated from Milan. It called upon designers to look broadly at their profession; to design everything from "a spoon to a city." Massimo Vignelli, then an architecture student at the University of Milan, was deeply affected by these stirrings. Eventually, they led him to every conceivable corner of design.

During this time, Vignelli became friends with the Swiss graphic designer **Max Huber,** who introduced him to Swiss methodology and the basic elements of graphic design: namely the typographic grid, sequencing, and dynamic scale relationships. Huber's objective and elemental approach was new to Italy, and through it, Vignelli came to understand the communicative potential of graphic design. The work and writings of two other Swiss designers, **Max Bill** and **Josef Muller-Brockmann,** also increased Vignelli's understanding of objective visual design and typographic structure.

American influences were also present in Milan. Every month Vignelli would pore over *Esquire* magazine, examining **Henry Wolf's** very personal approach to type, white space, and expressive photography. American designers **Saul Bass** and **Gyorgy Kepes** also stirred his imagination. Later, the German designer **Willy Fleckhouse** and his daring *Twen* magazine opened new vistas for magazine design. Scale and sequence suddenly took on new meaning for Vignelli.

Of Vignelli's many resources, architecture has been the most important guideline and reference in his typographic work. Through it he became fascinated with typographic structure and the integration of type and architecture. "Brunelleschi and Palladio have been more inspirational and seminal than any example of typography in the past, with Bodoni being the only exception. Bodoni belongs to the neoclassical tradition at the height of its revival and expresses it in sublime form. The intensity of the typefaces, the elegance of the proportions, the rigorousness of his typographical compositions have been a platform on which my aesthetic education took shape . . . but most of all,"

1 Poster for the 31st Biennale of Art in Venice.

2 Covers for *Skyline* magazine.

2

Vignelli reflects, "**Mies van der Rohe** has been the most influential figure in my formation. His poetry, essentiality, and sublime elegance have been a constant guide to my entire work."

With Vignelli's education rooted in the **Renaissance** and the **Bauhaus,** it is no surprise that he is a classicist in love with logic and order. And although Vignelli's work cannot be associated with a style per se, one may observe specific qualities in his work: visual rationality, objective functionality, and sleek, geometrical simplicity.

In 1965 Vignelli left Milan and moved to New York. An earlier visit had convinced him that America was a design frontier, a place where vision was grand and opportunities endless. Since his arrival Vignelli has left an indelible mark on American design. Emilio Ambasz, Curator of Design at the Museum of Modern Art, states: "Almost single-handedly Massimo introduced and imposed the Helvetica typeface throughout the vast two-dimensional landscape of corporate America."

According to Vignelli, three things are needed for effective design: discipline, appropriateness, and ambiguity. Discipline brings consistency and structure to a problem, relating parts to the whole; appropriateness is the quest for a specific and suitable solution to the problem; and ambiguity arises when two or more possible meanings tug at the mind. An invitation printed on tissue paper for an exhibition of

Massimo Vignelli (born in 1931 in Milan, Italy) studied architecture in Milan and Venice. He works with his wife, Lella, an architect, in the design of corporate identity and graphic programs, transportation and architectural graphics, exhibitions and interiors, furniture, and a variety of products. He has lectured on design throughout the world, is a member of the AGI, and is a past President of the American Institute of Graphic Arts. Recent major awards include the 1983 Gold Medal of the AIGA, and the first Presidential Design Award, 1985.

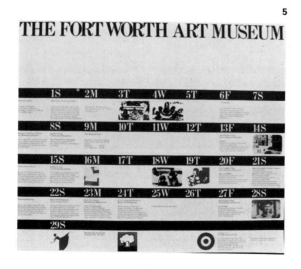

3   Covers for Sansoni Books, Florence, Italy.

4   Poster for the Piccolo Teatro of Milan.

5   Calendar for the Fort Worth Art Museum.

Massimo Vignelli

6

Vignelli's work clearly demonstrates the latter idea (Fig. 6). An elegant, classical design features centered, Bodoni type in all capitals. The message sent by this visual code is destroyed when the paper is crumpled — distorting the type, and mocking the classicism. The viewer is forced into a mental dialogue: Is it new, or is it old? Is it serious, or is it a joke?

Whether Vignelli is involved with a mammoth project such as a graphic system for the New York subway, or a shopping bag for Bloomingdale's, his first concern is to establish a visual code that leads a reader to understand the intended message. His second consideration is to articulate a hierarchy of information by identifying functional units (headlines, primary text, subordinate text), and to organize these units into appropriate spatial contexts (size, weight, placement). An early example that demonstrates Vignelli's concern for information hierarchy is his design of the graphic format of the Piccolo Teatro of Milan (Fig. 4). Here he introduced the concept of "information bands," which became an important aspect of his design in the years that followed. Thick black stripes separate the bands, while red and black colors help to organize the different parts of the message into a whole. Over the years, this concept has extremely influenced many other designers. For consistency and clarity, Vignelli can almost count on one hand the typefaces he finds appropriate: Bodoni, Garamond, Century Expanded, Times Roman, Helvetica, and Futura. He disapproves of the typefaces that do not reflect historical integrity.

Vignelli has kept an auto-focused eye on the way his work has evolved throughout the years. He recalls the early sixties when he was mostly concerned about the notion of objectivity and timelessness in design. "We learned in the seventies that there's more than one ideology that you can respect. You don't have to do things the same way all the time. You can consider alternatives. Now we're in the decade of the eighties, a time of probing. The risk of the unknown is much more exciting than the security of the known. But it will take courage to go beyond the usual graphics to express that new spirit."

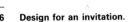

6   Design for an invitation.

7,8   Cover and interior spread from
The Audubon Society Nature Guides.

9   Various publications designed by
Massimo Vignelli.

7

THE AUDUBON SOCIETY BOOK OF WILDFLOWERS
A Photographic Celebration of Unspoiled America
the WILD PLACES
SKYLINE
A Narrative History of the Portrait in Photography by Ben Maddow
Faces
SKYLINE
The Architecture and Design Review
AMERICAN HERITAGE
Knoll au Louvre
Eric Larrabee Massimo Vignelli
Knoll Design
The Audubon Society Field Guide to North American Wildflowers
The Audubon Society Field Guide to North American Butterflies
The Mountains of America
Peter Eisenman
HOUSE X
Rizzoli
Graphic Design for Non-Profit Organizations

102

103

8

9

Debra Weier

1   2

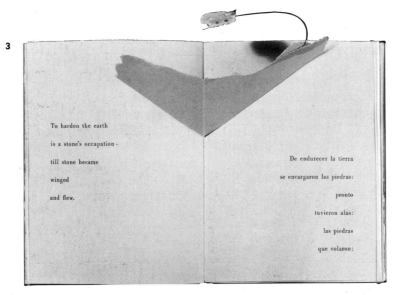

3

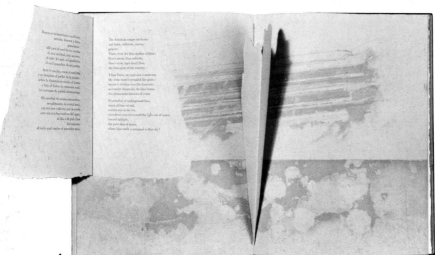

4

Debra Weier demonstrates that book design, after nearly five hundred years of development, is still in its infancy. She makes books by hand that jolt the most dedicated of connoisseurs, challenge the most scrupulous of readers, and gratify the most cynical of critics. Her books—landmarks by which the future of the medium can be assessed—would meet the strict approval of Aldus Manutius, the fifteenth-century master of **Renaissance** typography and book design.

Weier's interest in typography and book design deepened during study with **Walter Hamady** of Perishable Press Ltd. Before students worked with type, Hamady required them to make a series of one-of-a-kind, wordless "books" dealing with the sequential picture plane. From this telling experience Weier found the book to be a kinetic medium, much like film, wherein all elements must be integrated into a continuous and unified whole. As time passed, she perfected her typographic sensibilities and explored the sculptural possibilities of the book.

In 1976, Weier established the Emanon Press. Collaborating with poets, she makes limited-edition, labor-intensive books combining both conventional and off-the-wall materials, techniques, and processes. The opening of the press marked the beginning of her participation in a new American **book-art** movement—a movement

dedicated to the preservation and advancement of book design and typography. Abuse of technology is a looming threat to the personalized book, and while this valued symbol of culture may not survive as a major carrier of functional information, being replaced by massive data banks of digital tangles, it will thrive as a major art form. Weier sees book-art to be an arbitrator between old and new technologies.

For inspiration, Weier turns to a number of sources. Among these are illuminated manuscripts such as *The Book of Kells* and Japanese scrolls. The scrolls have taught her that words and images must be integrated with a sense of rhythm, recurrence, and sequential flow; for this is the nature of the book. She is also

Debra Weier (born in 1954 in West Bend, Wisconsin) received a BFA in 1976 and an MFA in 1979 in painting and printmaking from the University of Wisconsin, Madison. In 1977 she founded the Emanon Press, which is devoted to designing and publishing fine limited-edition books. Her work is in numerous collections, including the Library of Congress, the Brooklyn Museum of Art, the British Museum, London, the Metropolitan Museum of Art, New York, and the New York Public Library. An extensive list of awards and exhibitions includes the American Institute of Graphic Arts Book Show.

5

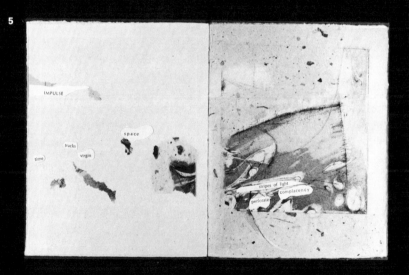

6

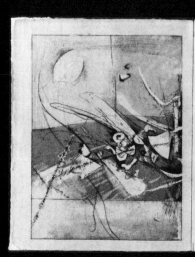
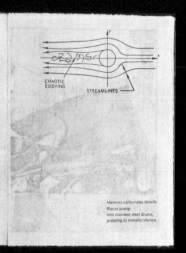

Debra Weier

7

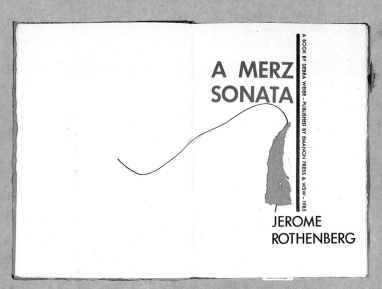

8

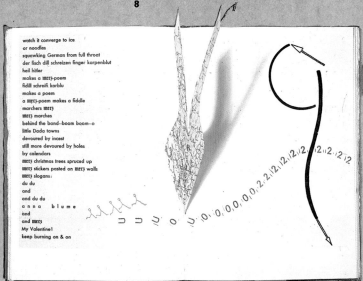

9

fascinated by the sensations derived from travelling through landscapes. *Skystones/Las Piedras del Cielo*, written by Pablo Neruda and designed by Weier, suggests continuous skyscapes and landscapes relating to the subject matter of the poems (Figs. 1–4). Six signatures contain etchings, various color stencil rolls, type-high plates, collage, and sculpted paper constructions that flow across gentle pages in continuous motion. Exquisite blocks of handset Bodoni Book type are concealed behind hinged paper flaps.

A Merz Sonata by Jerome Rothenberg, published in 1985, is an unpredictable visual experience for the reader (Figs. 7–10). The book is a tribute to **Kurt Schwitters,** the poet, artist, and graphic designer of Hanover, Germany, who during the early part of the century created **Merz,** a non-political, one-person movement closely related to **Dada.** Schwitters created powerful collage compositions from found materials including rubbish and printed ephemera found in streets and alleys. *A Merz Sonata* was created specifically with Schwitters' poetry and Merz compositions in mind: Rothenberg "collaged" into his poem bits of Schwitters' original poetry, while Weier "collaged" bits of Schwitters' imagery, literally and figuratively, into the book design.

Upon opening the book, one is immediately drawn to the end-papers. Gray, handmade paper, deliciously tactile, is embedded with bits and pieces of colored string. A collage of torn tickets greet the reader with "admit one." The title page reflects Schwitters' constructivist leanings with black and red type built onto the page at right angles. The hard edges of the type are softened with torn paper collaged to a length of string sensitively attached to the facing page. The result is a composition containing both whispers and screams. Inside the book, the poem is set in Futura (the word *Merz* is set in German Black Letter) on soft patches of color. The turning of each page offers a new surprise. Like snakes, sculptural pop-ups strike at the viewer then retreat mysteriously back into the book. Pictographic

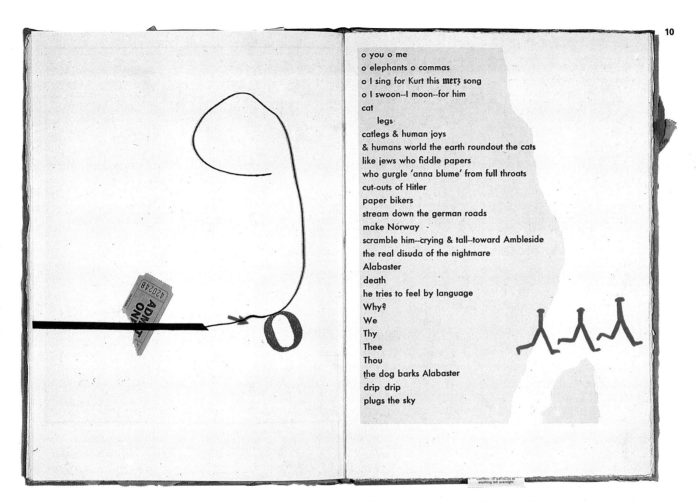

o you o me
o elephants o commas
o I sing for Kurt this merz song
o I swoon--I moon--for him
cat
    legs
catlegs & human joys
& humans world the earth roundout the cats
like jews who fiddle papers
who gurgle 'anna blume' from full throats
cut-outs of Hitler
paper bikers
stream down the german roads
make Norway
scramble him--crying & tall--toward Ambleside
the real disuda of the nightmare
Alabaster
death
he tries to feel by language
Why?
We
Thy
Thee
Thou
the dog barks Alabaster
drip drip
plugs the sky

rubber stampings, etchings, and collaged debris found throughout the book do not merely mimic Schwitters' work, but extend and broaden his original ideas.

These extraordinary books are the headwaters for future exploration and discovery. Unlike traditional books, they are forms of total expression made possible, in part, by Weier's design process: "I want the books I make to be living, breathing entities. The best way I can achieve this is to respond to the book as it is evolving, letting each new development have an influence on the next step. Some of my ideas come at the end of the production process when the book has already acquired a certain character. At this point the book begins to 'speak' for itself, and the artist/designer must be sensitive to this language."

Some of the best typography in America is produced by artists outside of mainstream graphic design. Weier's attitudes about typography align with those of such notable pioneers as **El Lissitzky, Theo van Doesburg,** Kurt Schwitters, and **Herbert Bayer.** These individuals placed no superficial barriers between the fine and applied arts. For them, as for Weier, visual language is universal and common to all artistic endeavors.

7–10   **Cover, double title spread, and interior spreads from *A Merz Sonata*, a poem by Jerome Rothenberg.**

Dietmar Winkler

During World War II, Dietmar Winkler and his family fled on foot from Plagwitz, Germany to the county of Bentheim, adjacent to the border of Holland, to escape the Russian invasion. His father was a well-trained academic and professional psychiatrist, his mother a talented self-taught artisan. While growing up, Winkler was interested in drawing and print-making; but because there was no art-related training offered in post-war German high schools, he was unable to study these subjects formally. To the dismay of his family, and its academic tradition, he spent most of his free time around carpentry, blacksmith, and mason's shops, fascinated by the tools and processes of the various trades.

After the war, cultural development in Germany lagged behind; the climate was one of uncertainty, non-commitment, guilt, and ideological confusion. In addition, most art schools considered typography to be a vocational craft of little consequence. Given these conditions, Winkler had to pursue typographic knowledge on his own after finishing his undergraduate training in design.

This process began during Winkler's employment with Chemie Gruenenthal, Gmbh as a senior designer. His responsibilities enabled him to work in the firm's sophisticated print and type shop, where he learned much about current typographic technologies and kindled a firm interest in typographic design. Information about form and aesthetics came mostly from outside German borders. "Distrustful of the German typographers," Winkler reflects, "which [sic] had flip-flopped in their ideologies, typographers from Holland and Switzerland (and a very few from Germany) were the strongest influence in my typographic development: **Piet Zwart,** Fritz Buehler, **Anton Stankowski, Jan Tschichold** among others."

At age twenty-one Winkler came to America to study at the Rhode Island School of Design. Here he met Alexander Nesbitt, a visionary teacher who, outside of a formal classroom setting, helped Winkler to see the value of approaching design from a broad point of

2

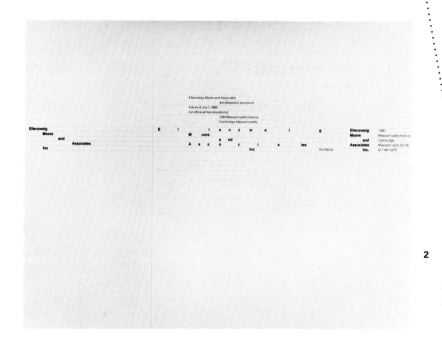

3

Dietmar Winkler (born in 1938 in Plagwitz, Lower Silesia, Germany) was educated at the Kunstschule Alsterdamm in Hamburg, and studied as a foreign fellow at the Rhode Island School of Design. Prior to becoming a professor of design at Southeastern Massachusetts University in 1981, he served as a type and design director at the MIT Office of Publications and the WGBH Educational Foundation. He has received numerous awards, and articles about his work have appeared in most major design periodicals, including *Graphis* magazine, *Communication Arts* magazine, and *Typo/Graphic*.

view: "He helped me to explore what the German schools had seriously neglected—an understanding of the integration between all components of a functioning epoch: arts, architecture, politics, and philosophical movements." Winkler soon became a student of existentialism, of **structuralism** and humanism; he read Sartre, Ionesco, Martin Buber, and Bertrand Russell. He combined this knowledge with an understanding of the great formgivers: **Le Corbusier, Frank Lloyd Wright,** and **Marcel Duchamp,** to name a few. Max Mahlmann, his teacher at the Kunstschule Alsterdamm in Hamburg and a non-objective, minimalist painter introduced him to the principles of concrete art.

"Structuralism" is a label that best describes the studio activities of Winkler. This term, which originally grew out of the school of structural linguistics, refers to language as a coherent system of formal signs with a specific systematic arrangement. Since structure is assumed to be the basis of all language, the term may also be used with confidence to describe the nature of visual language. In visual language, signs are

1   Poster for the *J.S. Bach Coffee Cantata* at MIT.

2   Announcement for an architectural firm.

3   Poster announcing a jazz workshop and concert at Brandeis University.

Dietmar Winkler

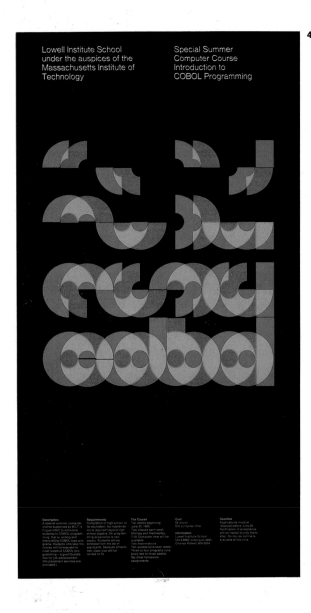

joined together to create messages, and it is the task of the designer to organize them into clear communication. This is illustrated in a distinguished poster representing computer programming (Fig. 4). Elemental forms — derived from specific parts of letters — are systematically assembled into a precise sign. This sign functions not only verbally as the word *COBOL*; it also functions visually as an abstraction of the programming process.

The typographic grid is used by Winkler to systematically bring order and clarity to information. One is reminded of **Josef Muller-Brockmann,** the Swiss designer and pioneer of the grid who said: "The use of the grid as an ordering system is the expression of a certain mental attitude inasmuch as it shows that the designer conceives his work in terms that are constructive and oriented to the future. This is the expression of a professional ethos: the designer's work should have the clearly intelligible, objective, functional and aesthetic quality of mathematical thinking."

While Winkler's work reflects these concerns, he sometimes finds it necessary to depart from the strict confines of the grid to intensify a message. A poster for the *J.S. Bach Coffee Cantata* features type — including the title of the concert, which appears in white Fraktur letters — floating freely as steam above an imposing pictographic image of a coffee pot (Fig. 1). A profile of Bach — also in white — is shown in reverse, corresponding to the title.

Winkler is a prolific designer, and his work has remained remarkably consistent due to a mature and far-reaching philosophy. Because he believes that the structure of the functioning universe is the ultimate model upon which culture should be based, he is continually searching for the means to more fully represent this model. This has led him to the discovery that "the more comprehensive the structural investigation, the more difficult and frail the solution."

4 Poster for a special COBOL programming course at MIT.

5 Poster announcing auditions and performances for *Utopia Ltd.*, by Gilbert and Sullivan.

6 Poster for a seminar at Brandeis University.

Brandeis University

Symposium in
Honor of the
Dedication of the
Ashton Graybiel
Spatial Orientation
Laboratory

Wednesday
October 20 and
Thursday
October 21, 1982

Open to the Public

Waltham
Massachusetts
647–2955

Man in Space

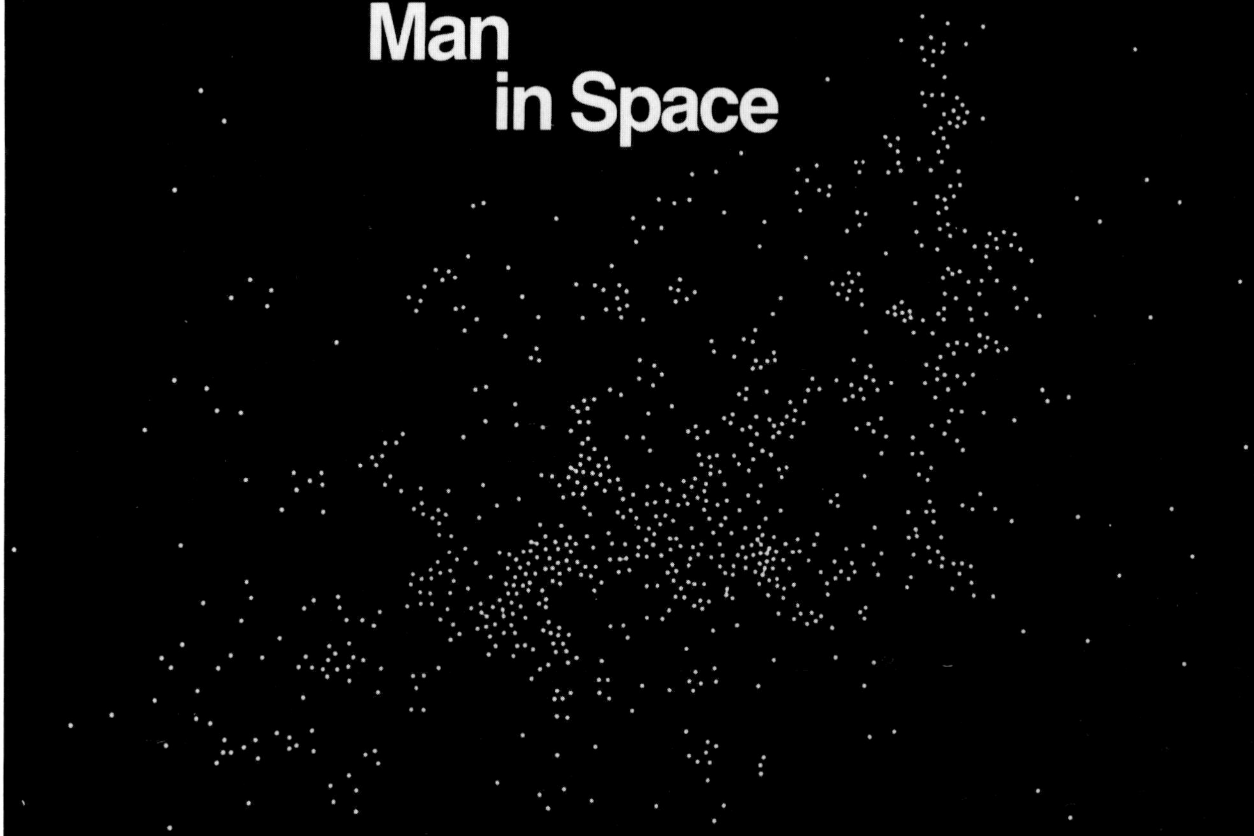

October 20		
9:30	Welcome	Henry L. Foster Chairman, Board of Trustees Brandeis University
		Anne P. Carter Dean of the Faculty Brandeis University
9:50	Introduction	Ricardo B. Morant Fierman Professor of Psychology Brandeis University
	Achieving Manned Orbital Flight	
10:00	**Man's Thrust into Space: The Evolution of an Idea**	Frederick I. Ordway, III Special Consultant Alabama Space and Rocket Center Huntsville, Alabama
11:15	**Inertial Guidance Systems on Earth and in Space**	Charles Stark Draper Institute Professor, Emeritus Massachusetts Institute of Technology Senior Scientist The Charles Stark Draper Laboratory, Inc Cambridge, Massachusetts
	Physiological Changes in Manned Space Flight	
1:30	**Anthropometric Changes and Fluid Shifts in Space Flight**	William E. Thornton Astronaut Scientist NASA Lyndon B. Johnson Space Center Houston, Texas
2:30	**Effects of Zero Gravity on Bone Integrity**	Leo Lutwak Professor of Medicine and Director of Clinical Nutrition North Eastern Ohio Universities College of Medicine Akron, Ohio
4:00	**Human Spatial Orientation in Unusual Gravitoinertial Force Environments**	James R. Lackner Meshulam and Judith Riklis Professor of Psychology and Chairman, Department of Psychology, Brandeis University

October 21		
	The Space Shuttle	
9:30	**Shuttle-Orbiter Flight-Test Medical Finding**	Sam L. Pool Chief, Medical Sciences Division NASA Lyndon B. Johnson Space Center Houston, Texas
10:45	**Space Lab IV: The First Life Sciences Dedicated Mission**	Bryant Cramer Project Scientist NASA Headquarters Washington, DC
	Man's Future in Space	
1:15	**An Augmented Program for National Aeronautics and Space Administration Vestibular Research**	Lawrence F. Dietlein Assistant Director for Life Sciences NASA Lyndon B. Johnson Space Center Houston, Texas
2:15	**Interstellar Travel**	George E. Mueller Chairman and President System Development Corporation Santa Monica, California

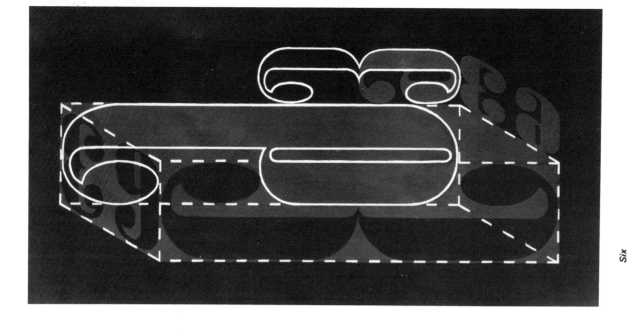

Josef Albers, *Six   and   Three,*   1931.

Adobe Systems, Inc. Developer of the page description language, PostScript. This language enables designers to use various design applications to mix type with images and print them with a laser printer or a high-resolution typesetter. The Adobe Type Library is rapidly growing with original and licensed typefaces. The company also manufactures a variety of software tools for the graphic designer, including Adobe Illustrator. Address: 1585 Charleston Road, P. O. Box 7900, Mountain View, CA 94039.

Dr. Mehemed Fehmy Agha (1896–1978). American art director and graphic designer. Born in Russia, immigrated to the United States from France in 1929. Dr. Agha pioneered the American magazine through his involvement in editorial decisions normally denied art directors. He considered all aspects of form and content, uniting typography, photography, illustration, and editorial content into precedent-setting page layouts. Immediately upon his arrival in the United States he served as art director for *Vanity Fair,* and later for *Vogue and House and Garden.*

Josef Albers (1888–1976). American educator, painter, lettering and furniture designer, and color theorist. Born in Germany, immigrated to the United States in 1933. Albers, a difficult and rather rigid man, became legendary as a design educator, shaping literally thousands of young minds over the years. In 1925, after being invited to teach in the Bauhaus preliminary course, he perfected methods for teaching basic design that have been imitated widely. He also experimented with lettering design; his systematic stenciled letters sought economy of form and material. In America he taught at Black Mountain College and Yale University, continuing to disseminate Bauhaus ideas and perfect his well-known color theories.

American Institute of Graphic Arts (AIGA). National nonprofit organization established in 1914 to serve the interests of the graphic design profession. The AIGA promotes excellence and advancement through competitions, exhibitions, educational activities, publications, and archival resources. Address: 1059 Third Avenue, New York, NY 10021.

American Type Founders Company (ATF). Established in 1892 by the merger of 23 independent American type foundries. ATF became the most influential manufacturer of foundry type during the first half of the twentieth century.

Guillaume Apollinaire (1880–1918). French writer and poet. Apollinaire was actively engaged in the avant-garde artistic movements at the turn of the century. With Pablo Picasso, he defined the principles of Cubism in painting and literature. His most significant contributions to typography are his experimental figurative poems called *Calligrammes.* He first called them "figurative poems" and "ideogrammatic poems." They consisted of letterforms unconventionally arranged into lively pictographic designs.

Apple Computer, Inc. Manufacturer of personal computer hardware and software, including the Apple Macintosh and LaserWriter. These tools, together with the PostScript page description language, made it possible in 1985 for desktop publishing to be born. Since then, the industry has grown at an unprecedented rate, irrevocably transforming the tools, materials, and processes of typography and graphic design. Address: 20525 Mariani Avenue, Cupertino, CA 95014.

Frank Armstrong. See page 16.

Rudolf Arnheim (b. 1904). Professor of the Psychology of Art at Harvard University whose classic writings have greatly enhanced the understanding of visual perception in all fields of art. *Art and Visual Perception* (1954), *Toward a Psychology of Art* (1966), and *Visual Thinking* (1969) are among his most noted works.

Jean (Hans) Arp (1887–1966). French painter and sculptor. Arp, the most gifted of the Zurich Dadaists, experimented freely with ideas of childhood

114
115

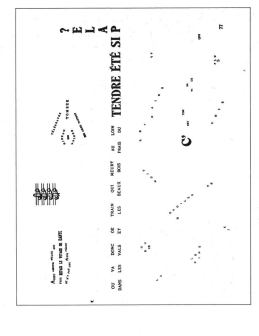

Guillaume Apollinaire, "calligramme," 1914.

Allgemeine Kunstgewerbeschule Basel. Design school in Switzerland that was originally shaped by the efforts of six teachers. They were Emil Ruder, Armin Hofmann, Robert Buchler, Andre Gurtler, Max Schmid, and Wolfgang Weingart. This school has been one of the most influential design institutions of the twentieth century. Kenneth Hiebert, a former student of the school, has said that, "The Basel approach to communication is structural. It relies on an analysis that rigorously questions and accounts for all parts of a message."

Alliance Graphique Internationale. International graphic design organization founded in 1951. The AGI differs from other organizations in that designers are elected to membership. There are just over 200 members from 24 countries in this graphic design organization.

Walter Allner (b. 1909). Graphic designer, painter, and educator. Born in Germany, immigrated to the United States in 1949. Allner was educated at the Bauhaus, under the guidance of Josef Albers, Wassily Kandinsky, Paul Klee, and Joost Schmidt. During his early career he also assisted the typographer Piet Zwart and the posterist Jean Carlu. Allner is credited, along with others, in continuing Bauhaus ideals in America. This is evident in his simple and concise designs for *Fortune* magazine, where he served as art director from 1963–1974. Major clients during his career have included Johnson and Johnson, RCA, ITT, IBM, and Container Corporation of America. Since 1974 he has been a professor of design at Parsons School of Design in New York City.

Alphatype Corporation. International supplier of type known for the quantity, quality, and exclusiveness of its type library and the range of its typesetting capabilities. Typefaces are designed "size for size" to preserve integrity and legibility, and extremely high resolution digital phototypesetting equipment is used to produce razor-sharp characters. Address: 7711 North Merrimac Avenue, Niles, IL 60648.

and chance so that he might perhaps reduce art to its most elementary, pure, and collective form. He constructed toy-like wooden reliefs from spontaneous forms painted in bright enamels, and created collages from torn scraps of paper dropped randomly into compositions. Chance operations had helped him to discover what he had always in vain struggled to achieve: pure expression.

Ars Typographica. Journal edited by Frederic Goudy and set in his types. Volume 1 numbers 1–3 (1918–1920) were published by the Marchbanks Press, New York; volume 1 number 4 (1934) was published by the Press of the Woolly Whale, New York. The scope of the journal as described by the publisher includes information on book and magazine printing, type design and type founding, the history and development of types and printing, and bits of curious typographic lore.

Art Deco. Decorative style popular during the 1920s and 1930s characterized by sleek geometrical and rectilinear shapes and the use of finely crafted manmade materials such as metal, plastic, and glass. Influences were Aztec and Egyptian art, Cubism and Fauvism, de Stijl and the Bauhaus. The familiar motifs of Art Deco—flowers, sunbursts, lightning bolts, and ziggurats—were used in abundance.

Art Nouveau. International style of decoration characterized by sinuously curved lines depicting flowers, vines, birds, and female forms. Art Nouveau was a modernist trend that rejected nineteenth-century historicism and attempted to treat ornament as an integral part of a design. Influences were Celtic ornament, Japanese woodcuts, Etruscan vases, and the Arts and Crafts Movement.

Arts and Crafts Movement. Nineteenth-century movement led by William Morris to counteract the social and artistic decadence brought on by the Industrial Revolution. Morris, an architect, designer, and writer, sought in the manner of the medieval craftsman to restore beauty to everyday objects by reuniting art with craft. His famed Kelmscott Press became a model for the production and printing of fine books.

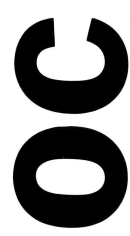

Association Typographique Internationale (ATypI). Organization established in 1957 with the goal of working towards an international policy that protects type designers from the piracy and adaptation of their work by others. The first president of ATypI was Charles Peignot of Paris, and later John Dreyfus, typographical advisor to Monotype. In 1973 at the Vienna Congress on Industrial Property, an agreement was reached when ten countries signed an "Arrangement for the Protection of Typefaces." Ratification of this agreement will take place when the internal laws of these countries are altered to reflect the content of the agreement. Address: P. O. Box 611, CH4142, Muenchen, Stein, Switzerland.

Theo Ballmer (1902–1965). Swiss graphic designer. Ballmer's posters bridged the de Stijl Movement and the International Typographic Style. He used mathematical grids to construct and organize geometrical letterforms similar to those used by Theo van Doesburg in 1919. Ballmer, a former student at the Bauhaus, taught design at the Allgemeine Kunstgewerbeschule in Basel for over thirty years.

Roland Barthes (1915–1980). French critic, writer, and semiotician (analyzer of signs). Barthes' writings about the nature of signs have greatly influenced the contemporary French school of thought known as structuralism (the investigation of sign systems). His writings reveal that all systems—whether sociological, cultural, or literary—are composed of signs functioning as language. His writings include *Mythologies*, 1957; *Elements of Semiology*, 1964; and *Writing Degree Zero*, 1968.

Saul Bass (b. 1921). American graphic designer and filmmaker. Bass is able to zero in on design problems, reducing images to simple but powerful pictographic icons. In *Man with a Golden Arm*, 1955, he was first to create a comprehensive identity program for a major motion picture, unifying both printed matter and film titles. He has created many ubiquitous corporate symbols that are fused into America's consciousness—the Bell System, The United Way, and United Airlines logos are among them.

Edward Benguiat (b. 1927). American type designer and lettering artist. Benguiat is one of the most prolific American type designers of the twentieth century. As well as creating many original typeface designs, Benguiat has revived many earlier forms. ITC Souvenir, originally designed by Morris Fuller Benton in 1914 is one example. He finds inspiration in everything from period type specimens to historical architectural lettering. To his credit are ITC Tiffany, ITC Korinna, ITC Benguiat, ITC Benguiat Gothic, and many more. Benguiat currently works with Plinc (Photo-Lettering Inc.) in New York City as a type designer and editor of the company's promotional publication, *PLINC.*

Morris Fuller Benton (1872–1948). American type designer and engineer. Benton has been called the unknown father of American typeface design. He created many typefaces that formed the basis of American typography. It was quite natural that he became involved in the type industry, for his father, Linn Boyd Benton, was one of the founding members of the American Type Founders and the inventor of the pantographic punchcutting machine. Many of Morris Fuller Benton's original and revival type designs are currently in use today as they were when he first created them for American Type Founders in the first two decades of the century. A small sampling of his accomplishments includes Century Schoolbook, Cheltenham, News Gothic, Franklin Gothic, Stymie, and Alternate Gothic. He also drew many excellent versions of classic types, including Garamond, Baskerville, Bulmer, Cloister, and Bodoni.

Henryk Berlewi (1894–1967). Polish graphic designer. Berlewi invented *Mechano-faktura*, a typographic style that banished any illusion of three-dimensional space from a composition. He produced mechanical constructions using simple geometric forms that reflected mechanized society; and in 1924, he founded Reklama Mechano, an advertising firm that adhered to the principles of mechanical space.

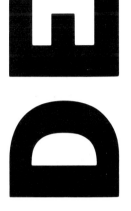

Morris Fuller Benton, Franklin Gothic, 1904.

Herbert Bayer, twenty-million mark note, 1925.

Bauhaus. Significant German design school founded in 1919 by the architect Walter Gropius. The initial aims of the school sought unification of all creative arts under the umbrella of architecture, and the restoration of craft as a fundamental. In 1923, the goals of the school shifted slightly to include a new thesis: "Art and Technology: A New Unity." This motto represented the lofty purpose of the Bauhaus before it was closed by the Nazis in 1933.

Herbert Bayer (1900–1985). American graphic designer, painter, and educator. Born in Austria, immigrated to the United States in 1938. Bayer was a student and teacher at the Bauhaus, responsible for establishing the Bauhaus style in typography. He consolidated the ideas of Dada, de Stijl, and Moholy-Nagy into a logical, but radical, approach to typography. He advocated the use of sans serif typefaces and, after 1927, the elimination of capital letters. He also used a variety of type sizes and weights to establish hierarchy, tinted boxes to emphasize information, and type positioned at right angles. In 1925 Bayer invented his universal alphabet, an experiment that reduced the alphabet to a single "case" of geometric letterforms.

Lester Beall (1903–1969). American graphic designer. Beall was the earliest American graphic designer to infuse ideas of the Modern Movement into his work. Called the American proponent of the new typography, Beall used an amazing variety of form—old engravings, wood type, photographs, and elementary shapes—to achieve functional design with visual contrast and rhythmic patterns. He produced landmark designs for the Rural Electrification Administration, *Scope*, and International Paper.

Peter Behrens (1868–1940). German architect, product and graphic designer. Behrens, a Jugenstil designer, is credited as the first to abandon the decorativeness of the nineteenth century for a simple, geometric, and functional approach to design. His work for the Allgemeine Elektricitats-Gesellschaft (AEG) became a guidepost for modern graphic design and typography. Through his former assistant, Walter Gropius, Behrens' influence was clearly felt at the Bauhaus.

Lucien Bernhard (1883–1972). American graphic designer. Born in Germany, immigrated to the United States in 1923. Bernhard was a self-trained graphic designer and pioneer of the modern pictorial poster. He developed a unique approach to the advertising poster by reducing it to a simple, brilliantly colored, two-part composition: a powerful image of the product composed of flat shapes and simple lettering carrying the product name. Bernhard also designed typefaces for the American Type Founders Company: Bernhard Fashion, Tango, Bernhard Gothic, and Lilith among them.

Berthold. For almost 130 years, Berthold has enjoyed the reputation of being the world's leader in all aspects of typographic quality. The company's typeface program comprises over 2,000 text faces with about 100 new faces added each year. The program is based upon adaptations of classical printing types that have been thoroughly researched, the Berthold Exclusiv program comprising the original designs of renowned type designers, and licensed designs from other sources such as the International Typeface Corporation (ITC). The collection is shown in a two-volume 1,500-page *Berthold Types* catalog. Address: 2 Pennsylvania Plaza, New York, NY 10121.

Charles Bigelow (b. 1945). American type and graphic designer and educator. Bigelow is a contemporary pioneer of type design who combines his knowledge of theory, history, and technology to create typefaces that meet the requirements of a new age. In collaboration with Kris Holmes he designed Lucida, the first typeface created specifically for desktop applications. For over twenty years he has helped to preserve native American languages by generating a written form of the Clackamas dialect of Chinook for the printed page. Syntax phonetic, a typeface intended specifically for Native American languages, was designed by Hans Ed. Meier, Bigelow, and Holmes.

116

117

Kunsthaus Zürich

FUTURISMO

FUTURA & PITTURA METAFISICA

November — Dezember 1950 · Täglich 10—12 und 14—17 Uhr · Montag geschlossen

City-Druck AG, Zürich

Max Bill, poster design for the Kunsthaus Zurich, 1950.

Max Bill (b. 1908). Swiss graphic, exhibition, and industrial designer, architect, and sculptor. Bill may be considered a primary link between the Bauhaus—where he was a student—and the International Typographic Style. His work, whether in architecture or typography, is based upon the universal principles of Concrete Art (absolute order and mathematical clarity). He was first introduced to these principles in 1931 after Theo van Doesburg published his *Manifesto of Art Concret* (1930). In 1950, Bill became director of the Hochschule fur Gestaltung (Institute of Design) in Ulm, Germany, where he evolved a post-Bauhaus, functionalist approach to problem solving. Eugen Gomringer, founder of the International Concrete Poetry Movement, was Bill's secretary at the time.

Joseph Binder (1898–1972). American graphic designer. Born in Austria, immigrated to the United States in 1935. During the mid-1920s, Binder developed a simplified pictorial style that established him as one of Europe's leading poster designers. He combined influences of the Vienna Secession, Cubism, and movements such as de Stijl and Constructivism into an approach that reduced images to simplified shapes. Pictorial depth was achieved by placing shapes of different colors side by side to create the illusion of light and shadow. After settling in the United States, he played an important role in the evolution of American modernist graphic design.

Bitstream, Inc. Digital typefoundry established in 1981 by Mike Parker and Matthew Carter. Bitstream is dedicated to developing and supplying digital outline masters for the desktop publishing market and imagesetters (machines that can both set type and print images) of all resolutions. The company is committed to restoring existing fonts that have been distorted over time, and to developing new faces as well. Bitstream's Fontware library represents a body of digital typefaces of impeccable quality. Address: Athenaeum House, 215 First Street, Cambridge, MA 02142.

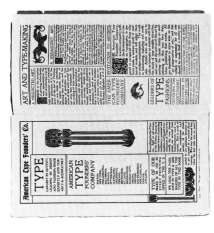

Will Bradley, advertisement
for American Typefounders Company
from *Bradley: His Book*, 1896.

Alexey Brodovitch, exhibition poster, 1932.

Joseph Blumenthal (b. 1897). American type and graphic designer, printer, and writer. Blumenthal was greatly influenced by the designer Bruce Rogers and the printer Daniel Updike, combining the skills of both designer and printer in his own work. He is well known for fine book and jobbing work done at the Spiral Press, and for Emerson, his only typeface design. His writings on typography include *Art of the Printed Book, 1455–1955* (1973), and *Typographic Years, A Printer's Journey Through a Half-century, 1925–1975* (1982).

Wilburn Bonnell. See page 20.

Book-Art. See Private Press Movement.

Will Bradley (1868–1962). American designer and illustrator. Influenced by William Morris and Aubrey Beardsley, Bradley's designs for the *Inland Printer* and *The Chap Book* marked the beginning of Art Nouveau as a graphic style in America. At the turn of the century, Bradley developed the "Chap Book Style" based upon his interest in colonial printing. The style was perfected in a series of twelve magazines entitled *The American Chap Book* designed for the American Type Founders Company. Also for ATF, he developed the Bradley typeface and numerous other type styles and ornaments.

Alexey Brodovitch (1898–1971). American graphic designer, art director, and educator. Born in Russia, immigrated to the United States from France in 1930. Brodovitch is best known for his influence upon the American magazine. He served as the art director of *Harper's Bazaar* from 1934 to 1958, where his innovative use of large, full-bleed photographs, refined typography, and rhythmic pages became the model for many other magazines. Brodovitch was also a stimulating teacher who, for over three decades, taught such people as Richard Avedon, Irving Penn, Henry Wolf, and Robert Gage.

118

119

A. M. Cassandre, railroad poster, 1927.

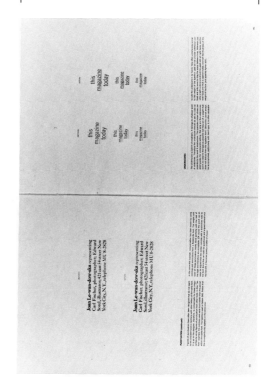

Aaron Burns, spread
from his book, *Typography*, 1961.

Robert Brownjohn (1925–1970). English graphic designer and painter. Brownjohn studied with Moholy-Nagy at the Institute of Design in Chicago, and in 1957 was joined by Ivan Chermayeff and Thomas Geismar to establish a design studio in New York. This partnership produced a wide variety of graphic design—album covers, posters, ads, and trademarks—that brought widespread attention. In 1960, Brownjohn left for England where he became known for his film title designs. The most memorable of these is the title for *Goldfinger*.

Lewis Carroll (1832–1898). English writer. Carroll received wide acclaim for his classical stories, *Alice's Adventures in Wonderland*, 1865, and *Through the Looking Glass*, 1872. His contribution to typography was the pioneering use of typographic form as a means to accentuate content—a device used effectively by Apollinaire, the Futurists, and the Dadaists during the early twentieth century.

Matthew Carter (b. 1937). American type designer. Born in England, immigrated to the United States in 1965. Carter began his career in 1955 in the Dutch firm of Enschede where he was trained as a punchcutter by Jan van Krimpen's assistant, Radisch. In 1965 he joined Mergenthaler Linotype in New York, where he designed a number of well-known typefaces including Snell Roundhand, Olympian, Video, Galliard, and Bell Centennial. In 1981, with Mike Parker, he formed Bitstream, a Cambridge-based digital typefoundry involved in the digitization of typefaces for the desktop publishing market.

Aaron Burns (b. 1922). American typographic designer. Burns is co-founder of the International Typeface Corporation (ITC), Editorial Director of *U&lc*, and author of *Typography* (1961). He is an advocate of typographic literacy who has lectured widely, and has assisted in the founding of several important organizations, including the International Center for the Typographic Arts (ICTA) in 1960, and the International Center for the Communication Arts and Sciences (ICCAS). As President of ICTA, Burns was a key figure in the organization of Typomundus 20 in 1965, the first international exhibition of twentieth-century typography.

Jacqueline Casey. See page 28.

A. M. Cassandre (1901–1968). French poster designer. Cassandre applied the principles of Cubism and Purism to the design of posters having the sole purpose of communicating clearly and concisely. Bold geometric images and refined letterforms were combined to convey accurate messages. As in Synthetic Cubism, Cassandre often introduced forms that functioned as symbols for his subject matter, rather than as representations of themselves. He also designed a number of well-known typefaces; Peignot, Acier, Chambord, and Bifur being the most popular.

Will Burtin (1908–1972). American graphic and exhibition designer, and educator. Born in Germany, immigrated to the United States in 1938. Burtin brought discipline to American graphic design through his scientific approach. He believed that visual communication was based upon four principal realities: the reality of man, as measure and measurer; the reality of light, color, and texture; the reality of space, motion, and time; and the reality of science. This philosophy enabled him to bring understanding to complex scientific information through his graphic and exhibition design. After opening a design studio in 1949, his most significant work was done for the Upjohn Pharmaceutical Company. For this company he designed *Scope* magazine and a number of exhibitions, including the ingenious model of a human red blood cell.

Chap books. Small, crudely printed books containing poems, stories, ballads, or religious tracts, sold by traveling chapmen (peddlers) in colonial New England. These books became a source of inspiration for Will Bradley, who, at the turn of the century, developed a "Chap Book Style" based on the use of Caslon type, spaced letters, simple rules, and bold woodcuts.

Warren Chappell (b. 1904). American type designer and illustrator. Chappell studied with Rudolf Koch in the early 1930s at the Offenbach

fccfcc phopho foorchtha   aggala   Jcesfice
                                    pAkoola
                                    ooridMiny
                                    afEared
                                    themSelves were to
                          majstate
                          nOr no
                          cruxwaY
                          no moorhens Cry
                          or moonEr's phankgang there to lead us
                                    Je m'incline
                                    mAis
                                    Moy jay trouvay
                                    la clEe
                                    dang les champS
sa na pa de valure whu's teit dans your Jambs
whur's that inclining and talkin abOut
                                    Your
                                    partmiCk
                                    diEudonnay have you seen her
by whydoyoucallme do not flingamefjg to the twolves
                          turcAfiera
                          aMd
                          Enough
                          wooluvS no less
                                    Jackstaff jerking
                                    why nOt
                                    saYs
                                    the frenChman i
                          was an orangEboat he is
                                    Jeyces
                                    sAys
                                    eMania
                                    watE him well
                                    acuShla
                                    animal Jangs
                                    hOwl me
                                    verY slowe
                          mirhyphalliC
                                    totEm

John Cage, page from
***Writing Through Finnegan's Wake*, 1978.**

John Cage (b. 1912). American composer, writer, and artist. John Cage altered the course of twentieth-century music by demonstrating that all sound is capable of being perceived as musical experience. Based upon the idea of indeterminacy—or the use of chance operations such as the I Ching—he attempts to heighten human awareness. He has applied this principle to his music, multi-media performances, art, and innovative typographical writings. In the mid–1940s, Cage taught at the Institute of Design in Chicago with Laszlo Moholy-Nagy.

Calligrammes. See Guillaume Apollinaire.

Calligraphy. Handwriting as a beautiful craft. The term implies a sound knowledge of the correct forms of letters, their historical development, and the skill to order the various parts of letters into harmonious compositions. Calligraphy has long been recognized by typographic designers as a tool with unlimited expressive possibilities. It was the basis of typeface design until about 1700.

Ronn Campisi. See page 24.

Jean Carlu (b. 1900). French graphic designer. Carlu is a pictorial modernist noted primarily for his posters. He transmitted powerful visual messages through the studied manipulation of simple geometric forms inspired by Cubism. These forms were often reduced to pictographic silhouettes and combined with lettering of a similar visual quality. In 1940, Carlu came to America where he stayed for several years before returning to France. Of note during this period are his posters for the U.S. Office of War Information.

Tom Carnase (b. 1939). American lettering artist, graphic and type designer. Carnase is best known for his masterful Spencerian scripts. He has created typeface designs such as Avant-Garde Gothic (co-designed with Herb Lubalin) and WTC Carnase. Fanciful logotype designs have been produced for *New York* and *Esquire* magazines, Grumbacher, and the Art Director's Club, to name a few. His typographic style is very similar to that of his former partner, Herb Lubalin.

Technical Institute, the result being his handsome pen-formed roman typefaces. ATF Lydian and Trajanus are good examples of his work.

Ivan Chermayeff (b. 1932). American graphic designer and illustrator. Born in England, immigrated to the United States in 1939. Early in his career, Chermayeff was an assistant to Alvin Lustig. This experience, combined with his association with his father, Serge Chermayeff, and Moholy-Nagy, provided him with a sound knowledge of European Modernism. In 1960, he became a partner in the firm of Chermayeff and Geismar Associates. Since then, he has applied his sense of color, texture, and simplicity of form to a variety of design problems. Chermayeff's poster designs, such as those for Mobil Oil, often consist of two primary elements: a provocative image and supportive typography that together reveal the essence of a message.

Seymour Chwast (b. 1931). American illustrator and graphic designer. In 1954, Chwast co-founded Push Pin Studio, an enterprise that altered the course of American graphic design. His work is based upon powerful concepts, a distinctive style of illustration, and an eclectic approach to typography and design. Chwast's vocabulary of form and color is based upon his appreciation of past artistic styles—Victorian, Art Nouveau, and Art Deco. He does not merely copy old styles; rather, he places them into new contexts and revitalizes them. Chwast has also designed novelty display alphabets for Photo-Lettering Inc., and Mergenthaler Linotype.

Classicism. Aesthetic attitude based upon the art and literature of ancient Greece and Rome stressing simplicity, proportion, and form. The Renaissance (roughly between 1500 and 1700) marked a revival of classical ideals. As art, literature, and learning were renewed, so were typography and book design. The brilliant work of Nicolas Jenson, Aldus Manutius, and Geoffroy Tory became the purest models upon which classical typography could be based. Their attitudes have been the focus of a similar revival in book and publication design during the twentieth century in America.

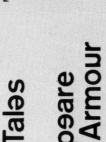

Rudolf De Harak, book cover
for *Twisted Tales from Shakespeare*, 1963.

Twisted Tales
from
Shakespeare
Richard Armour

Illustrated by Campbell Grant

($1.75)

McGRAW-HILL PAPERBACKS

Collage. Process of pasting found objects or fragments of objects—paper, string, cloth, letterforms, photographs, etc.—into compositions for symbolic and visual effect. This technique was made popular by the Synthetic Cubists, and further explored by the Futurists, the Dadaists, and the Surrealists.

David Colley. See page 32.

Colophon. Tabloid magazine published by Adobe Systems Incorporated. It features news about Adobe's products, including the Adobe type library, the PostScript page-description language, PostScript language software applications, and PostScript printers. Address: 1585 Charleston Road, P. O. Box 7900, Mountain View, CA 94039.

Communication Arts. Superbly printed magazine that spotlights the work of significant professional designers and covers a well-balanced mixture of topics, ranging from typography, photography, and illustration to advertising, corporate, and publication design. Four of the eight yearly issues are juried annuals representing graphic design, illustration, advertising design, and photography. Address: 410 Sherman Avenue, P. O. Box 10300, Palo Alto, CA 94303.

Compugraphic. Founded in 1960, Compugraphic is the world's largest manufacturer of typesetting equipment, with a type library of over 1,500 faces. These include Compugraphic original designs and redrawn faces, the entire International Typeface Corporation (ITC) collection, as well as licensed type from many other manufacturers. Alphabets are provided for several languages throughout the world. In 1985, the company introduced CG Lasertype for high-quality output on laser imagesetters. Address: 200 Ballardvale Street, Wilmington, MA 01887.

Muriel Cooper (b. 1925). American graphic designer and educator. Cooper has been a designer and teacher at the Massachusetts Institute of Technology for over thirty years. Her accomplishments include spearheading the highly influential MIT style of design as art director of the MIT Press, and pioneering design technologies as director of the Visible Language Workshop. Perhaps the most definitive example of her design is the landmark book *The Bauhaus*, by Hans M. Wingler.

Freeman Craw (b. 1917). American graphic, book, and type designer. Craw is primarily known for his numerous type designs, including ATF's Craw Clarendon and Craw Modern type families. He also designed CBS Sans, a secondary corporate typeface for CBS.

Cubism. Most important artistic movement of the twentieth century, established in Paris between 1907 and 1914 primarily by the painters Pablo Picasso and Georges Braque. Cubism emphasized the structure of objects by fragmenting them into angular planes and shapes that could be viewed simultaneously. Picasso's knowledge of Cezanne's paintings and African sculpture contributed to the movement. Two other artists of primary importance in the movement were Juan Gris and Fernand Léger.

e.e. cummings (1894–1962). American poet known for his lyricism and use of eccentric punctuation and typography. Devices such as the use of lowercase letters where capitals are normally used, and the bizarre spacing of letters, words, and lines of type, reflected his committed individualism. Altogether, cummings wrote twelve volumes, that in 1968 were combined into a two-volume set entitled *Complete Poems.*

122

123

paris 1925: grand honorary dipl. 2 gold medals silver & bronze medal-
paintings–plastic-wall panels–pillows–interiors–posters–publicity–stage settings

(handwritten note in Italian)

Fortunato Depero, writing paper with heading, 1928–1929.

Concrete poetry. Experimental poetry characterized by a wide range of approaches. It has been called visual poetry, pattern poetry, plastic poetry, and sound poetry. Themes have ranged from letters and words to collages, color, and found objects. The basis of any approach, however, is the physical material of language, its structure, and its reduction. In the nineteenth century, Lewis Carroll and Stéphane Mallarmé experimented with the visual effects of type in their writings. The work of early twentieth-century poets such as Guillaume Apollinaire, Ezra Pound, and e.e. cummings inspired an international movement beginning simultaneously in Switzerland with the poems of Eugen Gomringer and in Brazil with the Noigandres group. The achievement of the movement was in freeing poets from the bounds of traditional syntax.

Constructivism. Russian artistic movement influenced by Cubism and Futurism, and thought to have begun in 1913 with the "painted reliefs" of Vladimir Tatlin. The term Constructivism was derived from the *Realist Manifesto*, a publication written by Tatlin and his followers in 1920. In keeping with the new technological age, proponents of the movement were artist-engineers who "constructed" their work. Graphic design and typography were most influenced by the Constructivists El Lissitzky and Alexander Rodchenko. Moholy-Nagy, greatly influenced by El Lissitzky, disseminated Constructivist ideas at the New Bauhaus in Chicago.

Container Corporation of America. Founded in Chicago in 1926 by Walter Paepcke, a corporate leader who believed that design served both the specific needs of a corporation and the larger needs of society. In 1936, Paepcke asked Egbert Jacobson to serve as the corporate director of design. An impressive number of design innovators have since worked in CCA's design department. In 1952, with the help of Herbert Bayer, Paepcke launched the remarkable ad campaign, *Great Ideas of Western Man*. Some of the world's most important artists and designers participated in this effort.

Dadaism. Movement that erupted just after the beginning of the First World War with Hugo Ball's founding of Cabaret Voltaire in Zurich. The movement was prompted by a revolt against the values, traditions, and insanity that had led to the war. Members of the movement, in contempt for the public, attempted to shock and provoke by holding demonstrations, giving performances, and publishing manifestos alive with radical typography. They repudiated art, but this in a sense was a factor in the advancement of their art. They broke all rules, all conventions, and lived only by chance. Leaders of the movement included Tristan Tzara, Hugo Ball, and Hans Arp in Zurich; Marcel Duchamp, Francois Picabia, and Man Ray in New York City; George Grosz, Max Ernst, Hannah Hoch, Raoul Hausmann, and John Heartfield (Helmut Herzfelde) in Berlin.

Rudolf De Harak (b. 1924). American graphic designer and educator. De Harak is a self-taught designer partially responsible for launching the International Typographic Style in the United States during the late 1950s. His work evolved from rather musical arrangements of text and image to a formula of clarity and order: symbolic images combined with sans serif titles and informational text set within an orderly grid. Early in his career he designed over 350 book jackets for McGraw-Hill—work that epitomized his systematic approach. Over the years, he has also been involved with architectural graphics, exhibition design, and signage.

Fortunato Depero (1892–1960). Italian painter, graphic and interior designer. Depero was the only Italian Futurist to live and work in New York City, a metropolis that symbolized Sant' Elia's urban vision of the future city. The city, where he first stayed in 1928, was the ideological source of his work. Its energy, mechanical dynamics, and conflicting dimensions were embodied in his painting, tapestries, and graphic design. Both in New York and Italy, Depero operated a studio called Depero Futurist House.

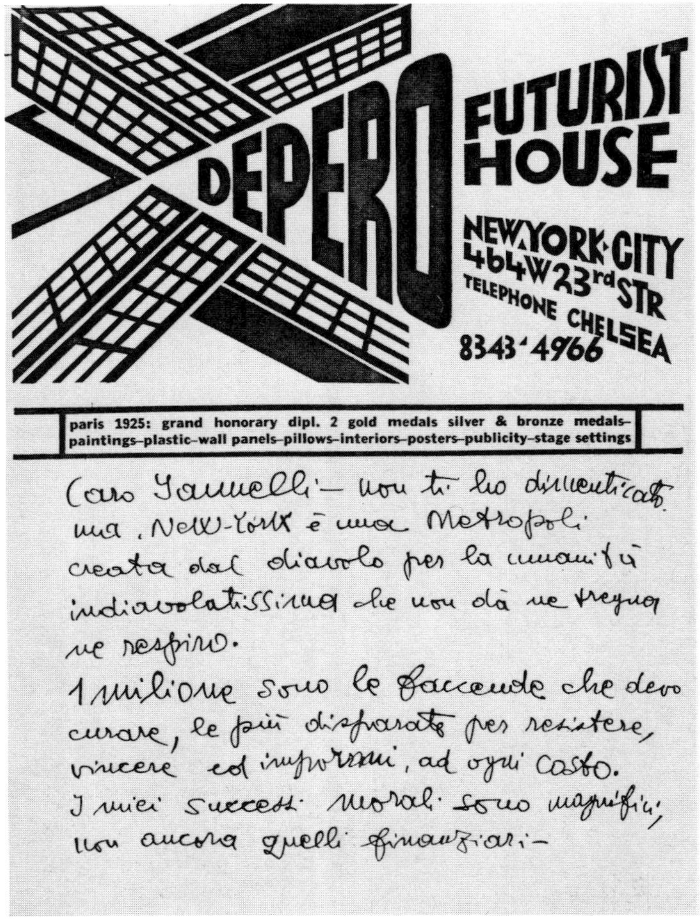

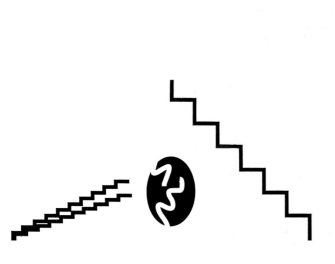

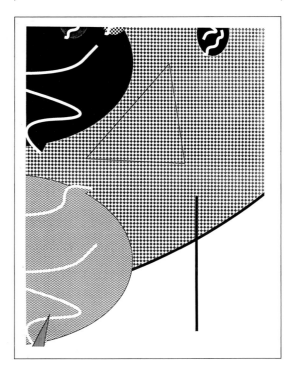

Douglas Higgins, page from a "desktop published" limited-edition book, 1988.

Ferdinand de Saussure (1857–1913). Swiss professor of linguistics. De Saussure was first to suggest the name "semiology" for the study of sign systems within a society. He approached language structurally, seeing it as a self-contained system of interdependent parts (signs) that acquire value through their relationship to the whole.

Desk-top publishing. Term coined by Paul Brainerd, the father of *Pagemaker*, a desk-top publishing computer program. Desk-top publishing, the process of creating publications directly on the screen of a microcomputer, came into existence in 1985 with the debut of the Apple LaserWriter. This device, driven by a page-description language called PostScript, enables high-resolution output of pages consisting of characters, shapes, and images. Desk-top publishing software makes it possible for a designer—while sitting at a microcomputer—to write text, specify type, create images, and layout pages simultaneously. This advance in technology is having an impact upon typesetting and design comparable to the invention of moveable type.

de Stijl. Dutch movement founded in 1917 by Theo van Doesburg with the purpose of refining the principles of Cubism and establishing formal laws of universal harmony through complete nonobjectivity. To achieve this, formal elements were reduced to horizontal and vertical shapes and lines; color was limited to red, yellow, blue, black, and white. It was a belief of the group that the laws of "pure art" could be applied to everyday objects, thus elevating everyday life. Active in the movement were Piet Mondrian, Bart van der Leck, Cesar Domela, J. J. P. Oud, Jan Wils, Vilmos Huszar, and Gerrit Rietveld.

Marcel Duchamp (1887–1968). French artist. Duchamp was a leader of the Dada movement, and a rebellious inventor who demystified and re-defined art. He proved through his work and lifelong example that art was a matter of chance as well as personal choice. These attitudes prompted him to paint a moustache on the Mona Lisa and to exhibit found objects such as a urinal as pieces of art. This revolt against artistic convention shocked and dismayed both the art world and the public, but forced them into a new way of seeing and thinking.

W. A. Dwiggins (1880–1956). American type and book designer. Dwiggins coined the term "graphic design" in the early 1920s. He is known primarily for the nearly 300 books designed for Alfred A. Knopf, and for eighteen typefaces produced for Mergenthaler Linotype. Of these typefaces, only five were made public. These include Caledonia and Electra (two of the most important typefaces of the twentieth century), Metro, and Eldorado. As a student of Frederic Goudy at the turn of the century, Dwiggins might be considered the last major remnant of the Arts and Crafts Movement.

Alvin Eisenman (b. 1921). American graphic designer, typographer, and educator. Eisenman has been a teacher and administrator in the Yale graphic design program for nearly forty years (1950–present). He is credited with having recruited as faculty such important designers as Paul Rand, Bradbury Thompson, and Norman Ives. He was manager of the design department of McGraw-Hill Book Company, 1945–1950; and typographer for Yale University Press, 1950–1960. He served as president of the American Institute of Graphic Arts from 1960–1963. Many of his books were honored by selection for AIGA's annual Fifty Books Exhibition.

Roger Excoffen (1910–1983). French graphic and type designer. Excoffen was an accomplished graphic designer who also produced a number of typefaces intended for use primarily in advertising. These include Chambord, Mistral, Choc, Diane, and Calypso. His most important type design is the popular Antique Olive, a highly refined and subtle sans serif in a class with Univers and Helvetica.

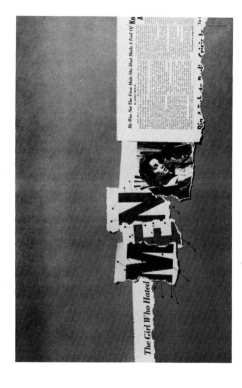

**Gene Federico, spread
from the *Saturday Evening Post*, 1961.**

Die neue typographie. Revolutionary typographic approach originating in the 1920s that applied functionalist ideas of the modern movements to graphic design. The "new typography" was first articulated by Jan Tschichold. It rejected ornamentation and anything artificial, it was purely functional, and it reflected the new age of the machine. Compositions were dynamic and asymmetrically structured, consisting of sans serif letterforms and other elemental shapes. Some designers were testing the limits of typography through intuitive experimentation. Piet Zwart, H. N. Werkman, Paul Schuitema, Ladislav Sutnar, Herbert Matter, Henryk Berlewi, and Willem Sandberg were among these.

Digital type. Type that is digitally encoded as a specific number of distinct points on a grid. Fonts are stored electronically as digital instructions to a computer. Because of phenomenal typesetting speed and continuous improvement in quality, digital type has revolutionized the typesetting industry.

The Dolphin. Limited-edition journal on the making of books, published by the Limited Editions Club of New York, 1933–1941. This publication consists of four volumes, the last consisting of three parts. In addition to *The Dolphin* serving as a showcase of fine typography, printing, and bookmaking, it is also filled with a wide range of excellent articles by notable practitioners.

Louis Dorfsman. See page 36.

John Dreyfus (b. 1918). British typographer, printing historian and lecturer. Dreyfus, a scholar of the highest order, designed books for Cambridge University Press, where he was Assistant Printer from 1949 to 1955. He also designed books for the Limited Editions Club of New York, to which he was European Consultant from 1956 to 1977. As Typographical Advisor to the British Monotype Corporation (1955–1982), he was responsible for their issuing types such as Univers, Apollo, Photina, Sabon, and Dante.

Expressionism. Artistic movement beginning in Europe during the early twentieth century that sought to convey emotional truth through the energy of exaggerated form and strong color instead of through accurate representations of the physical world. In a frantic search for self-expression, Van Gogh was the ripple that eventually set in motion a tidal wave of twentieth-century experiments by such artists as Wassily Kandinsky, Max Beckmann, Paul Klee, Chaim Soutine, and Willem De Kooning.

Fauvism. Art movement established in Paris in 1905 as a reaction against Impressionism. Fauvism is characterized by the use of simplified form and bright color. The term comes from the French word *fauve*, meaning wild beast. It describes the use of violent color by members of the movement. Raoul Dufy, Henri Matisse, and Georges Rouault were the major artists working in this vein.

Gene Federico (b. 1918). American graphic designer. Federico began his career as a graphic designer in 1938 after attending Pratt Institute, where he studied with Tom Benrimo. Lectures at the Institute also exposed him to Moholy-Nagy and Lester Beall. In the 1950s, his daring and unconventional approach to type, image, and space contributed to the birth of the expressive New York School of Design. He is a clear thinker who believes that typography should be tailored to the specific needs of a problem, and not just plugged into a tired formula. Federico considers himself a craftsman rather than an artist, and attempts only to clearly state his client's aims through elegant solutions.

Bea Feitler (b. 1938). American graphic designer. Born in Brazil, immigrated to the United States in 1961. Feitler was trained in graphic design at Parsons School of Design, and studied painting at the Museu de Arte Moderna in Rio de Janeiro. She served as art director of a number of magazines, including *Harper's Bazaar* and *Rolling Stone*. In the early 1970s, with Gloria Steinem, she formulated *Ms.*, one of the first magazines directed towards a specialized audience. Feitler's strength lies not in a consistent style of design, but in her ability to draw upon many resources to solve a variety of problems.

Eric Gill, letters from alphabets drawn for Douglas Cleverdon, 1926.

Frederic Goudy Goudy Old Style, 1916.

Louise Fili. See page 40.

Fine Print. Quarterly journal devoted to the practice of fine typography. This beautifully printed and typeset publication contains essays on typographic history and criticism, as well as reviews of books and exhibitions. Address: P. O. Box 3394, San Francisco, CA 94119.

Ian Hamilton Finlay (b. 1925). Scottish concrete poet. Finlay is acknowledged as the leading British exponent of the International Concrete Poetry Movement of the 1950s and 1960s. He continues to collaborate with typographers and stone and wood carvers to produce his standing poems (functional objects in the environment) and poem/constructions for architectural settings. He believes that if poetry is to function in the world, it must be physically evident in the world. For this reason, his work has been described as "typography in poetry." The basis of his poetry is paradox—opposing signs reduced to "silent" messages.

Willi Fleckhouse. German graphic designer and educator. As the designer of *Twen*—the magazine for mature teenagers—Fleckhouse made startling advances in magazine design. Although influenced by American magazines, his contributions brought a new sense of poetry to editorial design. Using provocative images—scaled beyond the boundaries of the page—and expressive typography, Fleckhouse created arresting page layouts that turned the heads of designers throughout Europe and the United States.

The Fleuron. Limited-edition journal of typography founded by Stanley Morison and Oliver Simon to examine the problems of type and book design, and to establish a common ground between printers, designers, artists, and readers. The first volume was published simultaneously in England and the United States. In all, a total of seven volumes of *The Fleuron* were published, from 1923 to 1930. The wide range of articles on all aspects of typography, and the superb quality of design and production elevate this publication to one of the finest typographic journals of the twentieth century.

Buckminster Fuller (1895–1983). American philosopher, designer, and inventor. Fuller, one of the most enlightened minds of the twentieth century, explored the future of environmental form with mathematical precision. Ahead of his time, he became well-known for his Dymaxion House (dymaxion = dynamic + maximum efficiency) of 1927; his Dymaxion Three-Wheeled Auto of 1932; and his geodesic domes, constructed of octahedrons and tetrahedrons. His book *Operating Manual for Spaceship Earth* (1969) was a factor in the launching of the environmentalist movement of the 1970s. It was Fuller's belief that humanity is capable of attaining a physical and spiritual view of the world through technology.

Futurism. Artistic movement founded in Italy by the poet and playwright Filippo Marinetti in 1909. Futurism sought to reflect in art and literature the dynamic quality of life as it was experienced in industrialized society. It glorified the motion and speed of machines, the danger and violence of war; and as well, it sought to destroy museums, libraries, academies, moralism, and feminism. Several manifestos written and published by the Futurists received much attention and influenced many artists and writers outside of Italy, including the Dadaists, the Russian Constructivists, and de Stijl. The five original painters of the movement were Umberto Boccioni, Carlo Carrá, Luigi Russolo, Giacomo Balla, and Gino Severini. Other important members were Ardengo Soffici and Corrado Govani, both of whom made important typographical contributions.

Robert Gage (b. 1921). American graphic designer. In the 1950s, a new approach to advertising was developed in the firm of Doyle Dane Bernbach; it stressed the interdependency of word and image. Gage, who was the head art director at the time, joined forces with copywriters to create concept-dominant advertisements using minimal but informative copy, and images that provoked attention. This intelligent approach was unlike typical advertising because it did not overwhelm the reader with inflated language. Of note are the ads created for Volkswagen, Levy's Bread, and Ohrbach's.

David Lance Goines (b. 1945). American graphic designer, calligrapher, and illustrator. Goines, best known for his poster designs, is a rarity among contemporary graphic designers. Not only does he design, illustrate, and letter his posters; he also prints them at his own facility, the Saint Hieronymous Press. Goines' work proves that a designer can draw from infinite sources, yet preserve personal style and vision. The trademark of his posters are images reduced to simple outlines, and images and period lettering accented with a hem of calm color.

William Golden (1911–1959). American graphic designer. In 1950, Golden created one of America's most familiar and timeless symbols, the CBS "eye." This mark is exemplary of the modernist ideal and standard of quality he brought to this major communications corporation, and in turn to the public environment. His participation with top management in making major decisions about corporate image was a pioneering step that raised the level of design consciousness throughout corporate America.

Eugen Gomringer (1887–1966). Swiss poet. Gomringer was one of the founders of the worldwide concrete poetry movement. He first became aware of the possibility of a new, more direct form of poetry while viewing concrete art as a child in Zurich. In 1952 he completed *avenidas*, the first of his concrete poems, or "constellations" as he called them. This term was borrowed from Mallarmé and used to describe the clustering of words. Gomringer's poems, which could be read in different directions, were precise, subtle, and restrained. Their simplicity and purity are reminiscent of the concrete art of Hans Arp.

Edward Gottschall (b. 1915). American typographer and writer. Gottschall was one of the founders of the International Typeface Corporation. Since 1938, his knowledge of typography—particularly the technical aspects—has been transmitted through his involvement in several publications. He has functioned as editor of the *Graphic Arts Yearbook*, co-editor of four *Advertising Directions* books, editor and co-publisher of *Art Direction* magazine, and contributor.

Thomas H. Geismar. See page 44.

Milton Glaser
exhibition poster, 1968.

Fluxus. International experimental art group founded by George Maciunas in 1962. Spurred by earlier twentieth-century art movements, Fluxus issued manifestos, published inexpensive editions of artist's works, and sponsored performance events. The group became an important influence during the mid-twentieth century, for it provided a forum for alternative thinking and challenged accepted notions of art and culture.

Adrian Frutiger (b. 1928). French graphic and type designer. Frutiger—one of the two greatest living type designers (Hermann Zapf is the second)—has designed more than twenty alphabets. From 1956 to 1958, he produced Univers, a remarkable contribution to twentieth-century typography. Renowned for its graphic unity, Univers is a typeface system composed of twenty-one integrated fonts. Each is identified by two numbers: the first indicates stroke weight; the second refers to the width of letters. Roman faces are designated by odd numbers; oblique faces by even numbers. The Univers family ranges from Univers 83 (expanded/extrabold) to Univers 39 (light/extra condensed). The normal book face is Univers 55. Other typefaces designed by Frutiger include Serifa, Egyptienne, Meridien, and Frutiger.

Functionalism. Doctrine stating that the function of an object should determine its design and materials; it stresses purpose, utility, and practicality. Functionalism became the philosophical basis and overriding concern in all areas of modern design.

Karl Gerstner (b. 1930). Swiss graphic designer and painter. Gerstner, influenced by Bauhaus philosophy, considers himself a "picture-maker," and throughout the years has attempted to systematize design, or more aptly put, to seek programs for solutions. He has written numerous books examining these theories, the best known being *Designing Programs*, and *Compendium for Literates*. The latter book attempts a systematic approach to typography.

Gestalt psychology. School of psychology that relies upon scientific experiments to reveal the mysteries of perceptual organization. Gestalt theory asserts that meaning is derived only if parts become a whole. In an essay by Christian von Ehrenfels, a clear analogy is given: "If each of twelve observers listened to one of the twelve tones of a melody, the sum of their experiences would not correspond to the experience of someone listening to the whole melody."

Eric Gill (1882–1940). British type designer, illustrator, graphic designer, stone carver, and writer. Gill left an indelible mark upon the history of letterforms. He designed many widely used typefaces, highly expressive and hewn with a regard for the humanity of craft. He was a social activist who signed his name to many documents aimed at social injustice. His better known type designs include Perpetua, Gill Sans, Golden Cockerel, and Joanna. Gill's teacher and mentor was Edward Johnston.

Milton Glaser (b. 1929). American illustrator and graphic designer. Glaser co-founded Push Pin Studios in 1954. With other members of the group, he developed a relentlessly eclectic approach to graphic design that has remained intact over the years. Images, artifacts, and graphic ephemera are freely borrowed from many periods of the past and from a variety of present sources as well. Using innovative graphic techniques, he succeeds in bringing new life to old forms, establishing effective communication in the process. Glaser has designed a number of ornamental typefaces, including Neo-Futura (a stencil-like face based on Futura), Houdini, and Baby Teeth. These novelty display faces are less concerned with legibility than with curious effect.

sulting editor of *Graphic Arts Manual.* He is also author of the book, *Graphic Communication '80s* (1980).

Frederic Goudy (1865–1947). American type designer and writer. Goudy carried forth in America the last phase of the Arts and Crafts movement. Born in Bloomington, Illinois, he was exposed at a very early age to the work of William Morris and to books from other fine presses. Although Goudy was involved with printing until mid-life, it was in type design that he made an indelible mark. By far the most prolific designer of his time, Goudy produced over 120 typefaces, the most popular being Goudy Old Style. Other type designs include Camelot, Kennerley, Goudy Modern, Deepdene, and Californian. Inspiring and entertaining books written by Goudy include *The Alphabet* (1908), *Elements of Lettering* (1921), and *Typologia* (1940). Of note also are the two journals edited by Goudy, *Ars Typographica* and *Typographica*.

Diana Graham. See page 48.

Graphic Expressionism. Term coined by Herb Lubalin to describe the conglomeration of expressive design styles in America—particularly New York City—during the 1950s, and continuing to the present. This post-war school, though rooted in European Modernism, was shaped by America's diverse and individualistic culture.

Graphis. Bimonthly magazine published in four foreign language editions—English, German, French, and Japanese—that addresses international developments and trends in graphic design. Until 1986, *Graphis* was based in Zurich and for forty years was published by Walter Herdeg, a Swiss graphic designer. Address: 141 Lexington Avenue, New York, NY 10017.

Malcolm Grear. See page 52.

April Greiman. See page 56.

126
127

Armin Hofmann, concert poster, 1986.

Chauncy Griffith. American type director and designer. Early in the century, Griffith was responsible for transforming the Linotype Corporation into one of the world's greatest foundries through his cohesive, complete, and well-managed program. As program director from 1915 to 1948, he first revamped the newspaper types by introducing Ionic #5, followed by Excelsior and Corona. He had a good eye for design and always sought the most talented of designers. Also, he is credited with the design of Bell Gothic and Spartan. Starting as a country printer and Linotype sales representative, he became assistant to the president of Linotype.

Walter Gropius (1883–1969). American architect. Born in Germany, immigrated to the United States in 1934. In 1919, Gropius founded the legendary Weimar Bauhaus. As director, he handpicked some of the best artistic minds of the time to train students in the design of total environments. Gropius stressed teamwork, form and function, and a regard for new materials. These ideals were exemplified in his own architectural projects, including the Fagus Factory (1911), and the Werkbund administration building (1914). In 1938, he became professor of architecture at Harvard and established the Architects' Collaborative.

Walter Hamady. American book designer. Hamady is the proprietor of the Perishable Press Ltd., and a professor in the Department of Art at the University of Wisconsin, Madison; he teaches courses in bookmaking and fine printing. Through his efforts, the private press movement in America has been vitalized, for many of his students have gone on to establish significant presses of their own. Since 1964 he has published the work of modern poets (including his own writing), thereby promoting the widely accepted concept of modern poetry as the primary subject for innovative American printing. His books are often small and intimate; they are always highly experimental. He uses handmade papers exclusively (his have been named Shadwell), being one of the first in this country to promote their use. Hamady's masterpieces include *Hand Papermaking* and *The Wandering Tattler* by Diane Wakoski.

John Heartfield, cover for *Der Dada 3*, published by the Malik Verlag. 1920.

DADA

Hand composition. Method of setting type by placing individual pieces of metal type from a typecase into a composing stick. This method, which is essentially the same as that invented by Johannes Gutenberg in 1450, is extinct as a major means of setting type. It continues, however, to be used in the printing of limited edition books and experimental works at private presses.

128

129

John Heartfield (1891–1968). German graphic designer, illustrator, and painter. Heartfield, one of the original Berlin Dadaists, was a die-hard individualist whose original name, Helmut Herzfelde, was changed in 1916 to protest anti-English sentiment in Germany. Throughout his life he used photomontage as a means to send shock-messages directed against the evils of capitalism and fascism. He was also a typographic designer whose projects include *Neue Jugend*, a radical tabloid published by the Malik Verlag in the late 1920s that employed vigorous Dadaist typography.

Historicism. Term used to describe the heavy reliance upon, and imitation of, earlier historical styles in art and design.

Armin Hofmann (b. 1920). Swiss graphic designer and educator. Hofmann has been a guru at the Allgemeine Kunstgewerbeschule (school of design) in Basel for over forty years. As a leader of the International Typographic Style, he has emphasized the aesthetic value and communicative potential of elemental form. He approaches design and typography from a semiotic point of view, believing that meaning is derived through the interrelationships of signs. Hofmann's posters for the Basel State Theatre are exemplary demonstrations of these concepts. His book *Graphic Design Manual: Principles and Practice* (1966), has profoundly influenced graphic design education.

**Kris Holmes
and Charles Bigelow,
Lucida, 1985.**

Kris Holmes (b. 1950). American calligrapher and type designer. Holmes is a San Francisco-based type designer with expertise in the history of letterforms and the tools used to make them. She is the designer of Isadora and Sierra, and co-designer with Charles Bigelow of Lucida, the first original typeface designed for laser-printers. A trend of the late twentieth century is to integrate serif and sans serif faces into the same family. The Lucida "superfamily" includes serif, sans serif, script, monospaced typefaces, Greek and mathematical symbols. It is a system capable of clearly communicating a wide variety of information in a single document.

How. Bimonthly magazine featuring case studies on the techniques, processes, and ideas of graphic design, typography, illustration, photography, and animation. Address: 355 Lexington Avenue, New York, NY 10017.

Max Huber (b. 1919). Swiss graphic, exhibition, and industrial designer. Huber, who was educated at the Kunstgewerbeschule in Zurich, lived and worked in Milan where he became art director of Studio Boggeri in 1940. He returned to Zurich for a short time during the war where he collaborated with Max Bill and Werner Bischof on exhibition design. After returning to Milan in 1946, he produced work that influenced Italian design considerably. His designs often integrated complex photography, photomontage, abstract motifs, and striking patterns made of repeated letterforms, into dynamic compositions.

Allen Hurlburt (1910–1983). American graphic designer, writer, and educator. In 1953, Hurlburt became art director of *Look* magazine, where he remained for nearly twenty years. His asymmetrical arrangements of spectacular photographs and descriptive typography contributed to a remarkable, romantic era in the history of American magazine design. Four of his books have been widely used in the design profession: *Publication Design* (1971), *Layout* (1977), *The Grid* (1978), and *The Design Concept* (1981).

Institute of Design, Ulm. School of design founded in 1950 in recognition of the fact that "a place for research and training in the design problems of our time is needed. Such an institution has been lacking ever since the closing of the Bauhaus." Max Bill, a former student of the Bauhaus, was one of the organizers of the institution. When he was succeeded by Tomas Maldonado in 1956, the curriculum became increasingly dogmatic along scientific lines: "A good design has to live up to reality. For that reason, the work of the school must be done in conjunction with sociology, contemporary history, and other disciplines relating to our social structure." The school closed in 1968 due to funding problems.

International Council of Graphic Design Associations (Icograda). Organization established in 1962 to act as a non-political mediator between graphic design organizations throughout the world. The organization attempts to raise and establish standards, to promote excellence, to recognize achievement, to exchange information, and to develop theory and practice. Annual meetings enable designers, students, and practitioners of other disciplines to exchange information. An assortment of exhibitions and competitions are held in conjunction with the conferences. Address: 12 Blendon Terrace, Plumstead Common, London SE18 7RS, England.

Mathematical grid characteristic of the International Typographic Style.

Vilmos Huszar (1884–1960). Painter and graphic designer. Born in Hungary, immigrated to Holland in 1905. Huszar participated in the founding of the de Stijl movement in 1917. In this same year, he designed the first cover of *de Stijl* magazine, a landmark example of typographic design employing the principles of de Stijl. Sans serif typography asymmetrically composed in rectangular blocks, with red and black as the primary colors, characterize his work during this period. Huszar's formalist work, which was rooted in Cubism, expressed de Stijl's concern for universal harmony achieved through pure abstraction.

ID: *Magazine of International Design*. Bimonthly publication that covers all design disciplines, including graphic, product, and experimental design. One issue during the year is devoted to the *Annual Design Review*, an analytical report of significant design accomplishments. Address: 330 West 42nd Street, New York, NY 10036.

Idea. Bimonthly Japanese magazine that reports on the developments of graphic design, typography, illustration, photography, and many other areas of visual communication. Articles and examples focus on developed countries such as the United States, Germany, England, and Switzerland, and also the emerging countries such as India, Cuba, and many others. Address: 1-5-5 Kanda Nishikicho, Chiyoda-ku, Tokyo, Japan.

International Typeface Corporation (ITC). Founded in 1970 by Aaron Burns, Herb Lubalin, and Edward Rondthaler to design and commission typefaces for licensed distribution to subscribers worldwide. Many of the most notable international type designers, such as Hermann Zapf and Matthew Carter, have supplied ITC with original typefaces. Others are purchased from various manufacturers. The company also commissions designers to redraw earlier typefaces for new technology. Many of these revivals have been successful. However, a few have created a stir among graphic designers, for the names of some original typefaces have been retained while their forms have been altered considerably. Some of ITC's revivals include Franklin, Garamond, Century, Berkeley (an adaptation of Frederic Goudy's Californian), Korinna, and Souvenir (an adaptation of a rather marginal design by Morris Fuller Benton). The importance of ITC's influence upon typographic design in America is unquestionable. Address: 2 Hammarskjold Plaza, New York, NY 10017.

International Typographic Style. Typographic movement, also known as the "Swiss Style," that began during the 1950s, attained gale force through the 1960s and 1970s, and is kept alive by the purists of the 1980s. Practitioners of this style, believing that design is of necessity a socially useful activity, advocate a universal approach to design. Clarity, precision, and objectivity are achieved through the manipulation of timeless, elemental form. Characteristics of the style include the use of mathematical grids, sans serif typefaces set flush-left and ragged-right, and straightforward photography or diagrammatic material.

Robert Indiana (b. 1928). American pop artist. During the 1960s, Indiana developed a hard-edge painting formula—originally influenced by the work of Ellsworth Kelly—using flat geometric shapes, sign lettering, numbers, and symbols. With these ready-made formal elements he revealed the nature of American society: the motivations and aspirations, the materialism and spiritual numbness, and the rampant sexualized environment. His *LOVE* paintings and sculptures of 1966 are well known. Other Indiana slogans include *DIE, ERR, HUG, KILL,* and *YIELD.*

130

131

Wood type.

Norman Ives (1923–1978). American graphic designer, painter and printmaker, educator, and publisher. Ives was a member of the first graduate class in graphic design which began at Yale in 1950. He studied with some of the most prominent designers of the century, including Herbert Matter, Josef Albers, Alvin Lustig, Alexey Brodovitch, and Alvin Eisenman. Upon graduating in 1952, he became a teacher in the Yale graduate program, playing a crucial role in its development over the next 26 years. In addition to being noted for his graphic design, he created intricate and poetic typographic collages composed on grids; these are found in the collections of many major museums. As a publisher, he designed and produced portfolios on the work of such artists as Ad Reinhardt, Josef Albers, Walker Evans, Piet Mondrian, and Herbert Matter.

Egbert Jacobson (1890–1966). American product and graphic designer. Jacobson was the first director of the Department of Design at Container Corporation of America, serving from 1936 to 1956. His standardized design program for CCA greatly influenced corporate design in America. Advertisements reflected the quality of the company through strong visuals and minimum text. With Walter Paepcke and Herbert Bayer, he created the *Great Ideas of Western Man* series of advertisements, one of the most memorable institutional campaigns in advertising history. Each advertisement was the interpretation of a great idea by a well-known artist. Jacobson also designed CCA's second corporate logo.

Japonism. Influence of Japanese culture upon art, architecture, and design in America and Europe. After American Commodore Matthew C. Perry sailed to Japan in 1853 to sign a treaty that opened the country to trade, Japanese influences poured into the west. Japanese prints characterized by the simplification of natural forms, flattened shapes, decorative patterns, and flowing, calligraphic lines had considerable influence upon the Art Nouveau decorative style and upon the emerging modern movement. Fascination with Japanese culture has endured throughout the twentieth century in America, finding a home in the formal vocabulary of many designers.

Wassily Kandinsky (1866–1944). Russian painter. It is difficult to say who the first person was to make an abstract painting, but Kandinsky surely was one of the first to eliminate objects from his work. He labored intensely to establish a language of pure form and color that would reveal the spiritual in art. For him, art had no relationship to the practical needs of society. His ideas came from a mixture of sources, including the doctrines of Theosophy, Constructivism, Russian folk art, Fauvism, the French Symbolists, Bavarian glass-paintings, and Moslem tiles. He was a member of the *Blaue Reiter*, a group of German expressionist painters, and was appointed as a faculty member of the Bauhaus in 1922.

E. McKnight Kauffer (1890–1954). American stage, graphic and textile designer, and painter. Kauffer's most influential work was completed while living in England between the World Wars. His most important client was the London Underground Transport, for which he created over 140 posters. To these posters he applied the principles of modern art—especially Cubism—and the lyrical quality of the English landscape. They possessed both a painterly quality and a formal clarity. Kauffer's pioneering use of simplified form as expressive symbol is his most significant contribution to graphic design.

Ernst Keller (1891–1968). Swiss lettering, trademark, and graphic designer. The origins of Swiss design and its astounding impact upon European and American design can be traced to Ernst Keller. Although he considered himself primarily a lettering artist and calligrapher, he was the first Swiss designer to simplify and stylize images for intensified visual communication. His posters are the best examples of these experiments. Half of his life was devoted to developing the graphic design program at the Kunstgewerbeschule in Zurich.

Rob Roy Kelly (b. 1925). American graphic designer and educator. Kelly is well known for his book *American Wood Types* (1969). This important study and collection of early wood types contributed greatly to a renewed interest in these early forms among designers.

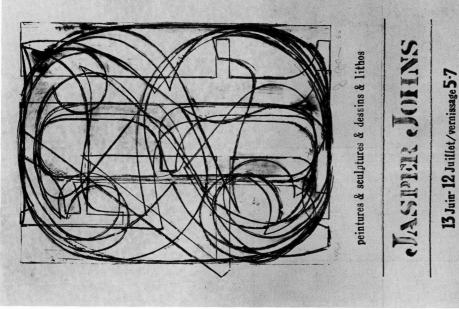

**Jasper Johns,
exhibition poster, 1960.**

Jasper Johns (b. 1930). American painter. In his paintings from 1955 to 1961, Johns used motifs so simple and familiar that he was able to work at unexplored levels of visual experience. The stenciled words and numbers, targets, flags, and fragments of human anatomy found on his canvases were not mere representations; they were signs referring to the reality of painting itself.

Edward Johnston (1872–1944). English calligrapher and type designer. Powerfully influenced by the ideas of William Morris, Johnston did more than anyone in the twentieth century to renew the art of lettering. He has been called the father of modern calligraphy, his model being the Harley 2904, a manuscript of the early Gothic period (late tenth century) in England. This manuscript represents a style midway between the Carolingian of Charlemagne's day and the Humanist bookhand of the Renaissance. In 1916 he was commissioned to design a typeface for exclusive use by the London Underground. The result was Johnston's Railway Type, a typeface of elemental construction. This design inspired Stanley Morison to ask Eric Gill to design a sans serif. Gill, a disciple of Johnston, said: "Johnston's influence was much more than that of a teacher of lettering. He profoundly altered the whole course of my life and all my ways of thinking."

Jugenstil. Late nineteenth and early twentieth century style of decorative art in Germany. *Jugenstil* ("young style") was Germany's version of Art Nouveau. Its name was taken from the periodical *Jugend,* which began publication in 1896. This publication and other forms of graphic design combined traditional German gothic types with Art Nouveau motifs. Practitioners of this style included Otto Eckmann, Hans Christiansen, Josef Sattler, and Peter Behrens.

Rockwell Kent (1882–1971). Painter, graphic artist, book designer, and writer. Kent was a politically active painter who also engaged in illustration and book design. His books, influenced by the work of Frederic Goudy, were strongly classical and enjoyed tremendous popularity during the 1920s and 1930s. He was well known for his boldly stylized woodcuts, which often illustrated his books. *Wilderness: A Journal of Quiet Adventure in Alaska* (1920), written, designed, and illustrated by Kent, is the seminal work upon which his reputation was based.

Gyorgy Kepes (b. 1906). American graphic, exhibition, and architectural designer, painter, photographer, and filmmaker. Born in Hungary, immigrated to the United States in 1937. Kepes is widely known and respected for his interdisciplinary approach to design and his sense of social responsibility. While never formally connected with the Bauhaus, his design philosophy and methods were similar in scope, and he worked as an assistant to Moholy-Nagy. *Language of Vision* (1944), a book developed by Kepes while teaching at the Institute of Design in Chicago, was a highly influential text for several years. From 1965 to 1972 he edited the *Vision and Value* series, a seven-volume collection of essays on various topics, representing the views of many disciplines.

Rudolf Koch (1876–1934). German lettering artist, graphic and type designer. Koch was to Germany what Edward Johnston was to England—a revivalist and reformer of earlier letterforms. Koch was powerfully influenced by the beautiful writing of medieval manuscripts, and much of his work reflected this interest. This is evident in handmade manuscript books created early in his career, in his handicrafts, and in his lettering and type designs. During his association with the Klingspor Type Foundry in Offenbach, he designed typefaces that ranged from black letter interpretations to grotesque forms such as Neuland and Kabel. Koch established a workshop of the Offenbach Technical Institute where he trained Berthold Wolpe and the American, Warren Chappell, among others.

132

133

El Lissitzky, title page and portfolio cover for *Proun, The First Kestner Portfolio*, 1923.

Willi Kunz. See page 60.

Gunter Gerhard Lange (b. 1921). German type designer and director. Lange, who was appointed type director of Berthold in 1973, has designed more than 100 typefaces for the company. His original typefaces include Solemnis and Concord. He is also responsible for the film adaptations of classical faces such as Baskerville, Caslon, Garamond, and Walbaum. His Bodoni is used by IBM as the corporate typeface. Lange has performed a major role in Berthold's leadership of typographic quality.

Le Corbusier (1887–1965). French architect. Le Corbusier, who called his houses "machines for living," was one of the most versatile contributors to twentieth-century architecture. His vocabulary was based upon two influences: classical buildings and the rationality of machines. While he failed as a sociological architect, he was a gifted inventor of form. This is best observed in his designs of single buildings, and epitomized in the Villa Savoye (1929–1931). This house, a white cube raised on twenty-six columns, is accented with a rich variety of features within its interior. It demonstrates Corbusier's concern for "the informed, correct and magnificent play of forms under light."

Fernand Léger (1881–1955). French painter. Léger was one of the early Cubist painters whose love of machinery led to his being called "the primitive of the machine age." He employed mechanical shapes to describe human figures and objects, assembling them into lively compositions of bright color. Geometric letters in his paintings revealed fragments of information and inspired the use of such forms in graphic design.

Warren Lehrer. See page 64.

134
135

Linotype. Machine that produces a single line of type to a predetermined length specified by a keyboard operator. Invented by Ottmar Mergenthaler in 1886, this machine was the major method of typesetting until the 1970s.

El Lissitzky (1890–1941). Russian painter, architect, city planner, graphic designer, and educator. El Lissitzky's contribution to twentieth-century typography is an extension of his theories of spatial dynamics, as exemplified in his *Prouns*. (This acronym for "Project for the Affirmation of the New," is pronounced "pro-oon.") These are compositions consisting of several two- and three-dimensional constructed forms that defy the normal expectations of spatial organization. In graphic design, El Lissitzky constructed "architectural pages," in which structure was determined by content and purpose. His greatest typographic achievements are the pioneering books, *Story of Two Squares* (1922), and *For the Voice* (1923).

Raymond Loewy (b. 1893). American industrial designer. Born in France, immigrated to the United States in 1919. Loewy "streamlined" America with his designs of everyday objects. He is famous for the diversity of his designs; for his comprehensive design services; and for his ability to link quality, efficiency, and safety with aesthetics. His aesthetic sense has shaped modern communication are as indivisible as Studebaker, Greyhound, United Airlines, Frigidaire, Lucky Strike, and Lord and Taylor.

George Lois (b. 1931). American advertising designer. Lois is the *enfant terrible* of advertising whose unique approach to advertising combines minimal but often humorous copy with effective images. He believes that, "An art director must be someone who treats words with the same reverence that he accords graphics because the verbal and visual elements of modern communication are as indivisible as words and music in a song." For Lois, advertising is as much an art form as painting. His famous ads include Allerest's "You don't have a cold! I dode hab a code?"; and for the Goodman Matzoh company, "I want my Maypo." He also produced many familiar covers for *Esquire* magazine during the 1960s.

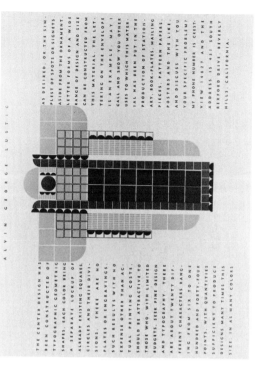

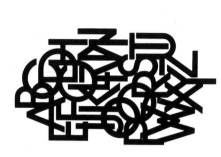

Alvin Lustig, promotion piece for the Lustig Design Office, 1937 to early 1940s.

Herb Lubalin, design incorporating all 26 characters of the Avant Garde typeface, 1967.

Letraset. Since 1961, Letraset has been a manufacturer of dry transfer lettering and a wide variety of other products, including audio-visual aids, shading films, color imaging systems, and Pantone color products. Rubdown letters have made it possible for graphic designers to create special effects by combining and overlapping forms without drawing them. Unfortunately, some of the novelty types in Letraset's collection are poorly designed, ugly, and often misused. Letraset offers effective tools in electronic publishing such as Ready Set Go, a page layout program for desktop publishing. Address: 40 Eisenhower Drive, Paramus, NJ 07652.

Claude Levi-Strauss (b. 1908). French anthropologist and philosopher. The central idea behind Levi-Strauss's theories of Structural Anthropology is that both "primitive" and "civilized" societies possess the same unconscious mental processes, and that these processes are tied to language. Therefore, cultural phenomena such as kinship, religion, ceremonies, art, and literature, may be analyzed as language, the primary signifying system among human beings. Structural linguistics offers a plausible model for such investigations.

Roy Lichtenstein (b. 1923). American painter and sculptor. Lichtenstein was a leader of the Pop Art movement in America whose subject matter was comic strips from the forties and fifties. Enlarging printer's dots was his way of removing an image from its original context to create a simple narrative sign. As a formalist, he was more concerned about the quality of the images (the textures of the dots, and the color) than about the subject matter itself.

Ligature. Tabloid magazine published by the World Typeface Center, Inc., New York. This publication, which is intended to showcase WTC's typefaces, is available free of charge. Regular features offer information on typographic technology and history. Address: 303 Park Avenue South, New York, NY 10010.

Herb Lubalin (1918–1981). American graphic and type designer. In the 1950's Lubalin received international acclaim for his expressive and rule-breaking exploration of phototype. He overlapped letters, enlarged them to outrageous sizes, and squeezed every drop of space from between letters, words, and lines. His innumerable typographic achievements include the design of word poems called *typograms*, of which "Mother & Child" and "Marriage" are familiar examples; his magazine designs for revolutionary publications such as *Eros, Fact,* and *Avant Garde* magazines; and his typeface designs, including Avant Garde (co-created with Tom Carnase), Lubalin Graph, and Serif Gothic.

Ludlow. Semiautomatic typecasting machine that combines both hand and machine production. Matrices are placed by hand into a composing stick where they are automatically adjusted for spacing. This is then inserted into a casting device whereupon it is cast into slugs.

Alvin Lustig (1915–1955). American graphic, interior, and furniture designer. Lustig was an influential designer during the 1940s and early 1950s who, as a generalist, designed everything from magazines to a helicopter. Possessing a modern sensibility, he reduced the content of design to basic form and color. He believed that "type alone can have power and taste"—an idea demonstrated time and time again in such work as book jackets for New Directions Books and Noonday Press. He was committed to design education, believing that it should lead industry and business. He taught at Black Mountain College, Art Center School in Los Angeles, and served as a consultant at Yale.

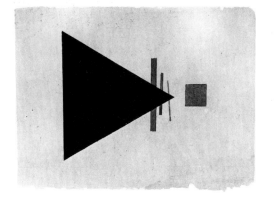

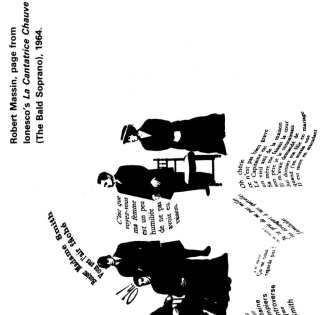

Kasimir Malevich, *Suprematism*, 1920.

Robert Massin, page from Ionesco's *La Cantatrice Chauve* (The Bald Soprano), 1964.

Charles Rennie Mackintosh (1868–1928). Scottish architect, interior, furniture, and graphic designer. Mackintosh is primarily known for his design of total architectural environments. This work, combined with a modest but superb amount of graphic design, renders him a profound influence on design at the turn of the century. He was one of four designers named the Four Macs (the others were Margaret Macdonald, Herbert McNair, and Frances Macdonald), referred to also as the Glasgow School. His strong rectilinear style extended the formal vocabulary of Art Nouveau by employing elongated vertical lines and accents of curvilinear and floral motifs, thus strongly anticipating the developments of the twentieth century.

Kasimir Malevich (1878–1935). Russian painter. Malevich is considered to be the first twentieth-century artist to leave behind the imitative subject matter of Cubism and enter the domain of pure geometric abstraction. His paintings, which he called Suprematist compositions, were first shown publically in 1915 at an exhibition called *0–10*. Malevich's philosophy rejected practical artistic applications for the supreme expression of feelings attained through the use of simplified form and color.

Malik Verlag. Avant-garde publishing house founded by Wieland Herzfelde, a Dada poet and critic from Berlin, and brother of John Heartfield. The Malik Verlag produced Dada literature and left-wing political propaganda.

Mannerism. Artistic style of the late sixteenth century characterized by the exaggeration and distortion of proportion and scale, classical balance, and the human figure. In a contemporary context, it refers to designers departing from established "norms."

Giovanni Mardersteig (1892–1977). German book and type designer and printer. Mardersteig, though educated as a lawyer, was one of the most significant scholarly printers of the twentieth century. With an abiding interest in Renaissance printing and letterforms, he developed a typographic approach to the page that was impeccably precise, yet sensuous as well. More often than not the magnificent books printed at his private press, called Officina Bodoni, contained typefaces of his own

Noel Martin (b. 1922). American graphic designer and painter. Martin, self-taught in typography and design, studied painting at the Cincinnati Art Institute from 1939 to 1941 and from 1945 to 1947. Later, as a teacher at this school, he inspired countless students through his example. Martin's work is lyrical, precise, and surprisingly varied. He possesses the ability to examine the formal qualities of letters with microscopic detail, resulting in puzzle-like compositions endowed with spatial harmony and graphic clarity.

John Massey (b. 1931). American graphic designer and painter. Massey believes that graphic design should be part of a "total environment." In 1957, after joining Container Corporation, he developed a standardized visual identification program for the firm that became a model for other such programs throughout the United States. In 1966, he established the Center for Advanced Research in Design, a subsidiary of Container Corporation. The Center provided Massey with the opportunity to develop identification programs for other organizations as well, including the Department of Labor—the first of such programs to be instituted for a United States government agency.

Robert Massin (b. 1925). French graphic designer, illustrator, and writer. In the 1960s, Massin became recognized for an approach to typography having affinities with Dadaism and Futurism, but which moved into new territories because of his unique, but faithful interpretation of an author's written text. To solutions of design problems he combines careful research, a sense of history, a refined intuitive judgement, and a love of classical letterforms. While art director for Editions Gallimard from 1958 to 1978, he produced the work for which he is best known, including his designs for Ionesco's plays. Several years of typographic research culminated in *Letter and Image* (1970), a book exploring letterforms as they have been used throughout the ages.

Herbert Matter, travel poster for Switzerland, 1936.

design. These include Zeno and Dante. The latter face, eventually produced by Monotype Corporation, represents one of his most profound achievements.

Michael Manwaring. See page 68.

Aaron Marcus. American graphic designer and scientist. Since the 1960s, Marcus has explored the interrelationship between new technology and visual language. Many of his experiments have probed the nature of typographic form as both a practical and poetic medium. He says, "The computer's architecture of information makes us freer than ever before to create forms, to move around, twist and turn, to create markings and symbolic monuments, to produce something as animated as a ferris wheel at a carnival, or as static as a cemetery." Influences include early twentieth-century poets such as Apollinaire, and the international concrete poetry movement.

Filippo Marinetti (1876–1944). Italian writer. Marinetti, the founder of Futurism, was obsessed with destroying traditional values and with revealing the energy of the new machine age in art and literature; "dynamism" and "simultaneity" were his weapons. The Futurist Manifesto, written by Marinetti in 1909, best exemplifies his doctrine. It proclaims that "the world's splendor has been enriched by a new beauty: the beauty of speed . . . A roaring automobile, which seems to operate like a machine gun, is more beautiful than the *Winged Victory of Samothrace*. "War," he asserted, "is the only cure for the world." In 1913, Marinetti wrote his second technical manifesto entitled *Destruction of Syntax, Imagination Without Sequence, Words in Liberty*, that began a typographical revolution of considerable consequence to artists and designers throughout Europe.

Henri Matisse (1869–1954). French painter and sculptor. Matisse may be counted among the great radical artists of this century. From 1905 to 1908 he led the Fauvist movement as a revolutionary colorist. From work during these years, he developed his characteristic simplified style in which objects and backgrounds became flat, decorative patterns. In the 1950s, he carried art into new realms by cutting large sheets of colored paper into flat objects collaged together. Perhaps no other artist has been as widely imitated by late twentieth-century graphic designers as Matisse.

Matrix. Annual limited-edition review of fine printing, typography, and the art of the book. *Matrix* features provocative articles, is stunningly printed by letterpress, and contains tipped-in and bound-in illustrations. It has been printed since 1981 by the Wittington Press in Gloucestershire, England.

Herbert Matter (1907–1984). American graphic designer and photographer. Born in Switzerland, immigrated to the United States in 1936. Early in his career, Matter studied painting with Fernand Léger and later worked for A. M. Cassandre and Le Corbusier in Paris. While in Paris he developed an interest in photography, typography, and poster design—interests that evolved into his Swiss travel posters, for which he received wide acclaim. These posters are characterized by dramatic scale relationships and surrealistic photomontage techniques. In America, Matter was a consultant to Knoll Associates, and for twenty-five years taught photography at Yale University.

Marshall McLuhan (1911–1981). Canadian literary critic and communications sociologist. McLuhan was the prophet of the idea that media, such as print and television, influence and sometimes overshadow the messages they send. He asserted that the instant information of television would transform the world into a global village. His books include *The Medium is the Message* (1967).

Mechano-faktura. See Henryk Berlewi.

136
137

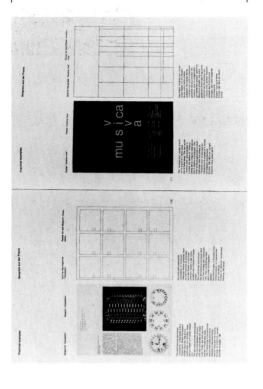

Josef Muller-Brockmann, interior spread from his book, *Grid Systems in Graphic Design*, 1981.

BAUHAUSBÜCHER

SCHRIFTLEITUNG:
WALTER GROPIUS
L. MOHOLY-NAGY

L. MOHOLY-NAGY:
MALEREI, PHOTOGRAPHIE, FILM

8

L. MOHOLY-NAGY:
MALEREI
PHOTOGRAPHIE
FILM

ALBERT LANGEN VERLAG MÜNCHEN

Laszlo Moholy-Nagy, title spread from Bauhaus Book 8, 1925.

Medieval Era. Period in European history sandwiched between the fall of the Roman Empire (fifth century A.D.) and the beginning of the Renaissance (fifteenth century). During this one-thousand year "dark" period, in which most of the learning and knowledge of the classical world had been lost, a rich tradition of book making evolved from a combination of Roman and pagan sources. Christian monasteries became cultural centers, and it was here that beautiful illuminated manuscripts were made for the preservation of knowledge. Letterforms developed during the late Medieval period became models for typeface design after the discovery of moveable type. Manuscripts that continue to amaze and inspire are *The Book of Kells, The Douce Apocalypse,* and *The Ormesby Psalter.*

Mergenthaler Linotype. Manufacturer of the first line-casting typesetter invented by Ottmar Mergenthaler in 1886. Now, over 100 years later, the company produces Linotron CRT digital typesetters, and Linotronic laser imagesetters that set type from Linotype Laser Fonts. Over 1,600 of these fonts are found in the Mergenthaler Type Library. Linotype's imagesetters accept input from almost all major front-end systems and many personal computers. They enable graphic designers to obtain high resolution output for work produced on desktop publishing systems. The company also produces down-loadable PostScript fonts for direct use with small personal design stations such as Apple Macintosh computers. Address: 425 Oser Avenue, Hauppauge, NY 11788.

Merz. See Kurt Schwitters.

Robert Hunter Middleton (1898–1985). American type designer. Born in Scotland, immigrated to the United States in 1908. For most of his working life, Middleton was a designer and design director of the Ludlow Typograph Company of Chicago. He was a highly respected designer and craftsman, developing a large number of practical typefaces during his career. These include Eusebius, a roman modelled after the types of the Renaissance designer Nicolas Jenson; a Garamond and a Bodoni; Ludlow Black; Tempo, a sans serif similar to Futura; and Stellar, a sans serif roman similar in quality to Hermann Zapf's Optima.

Piet Mondrian (1872–1944). Dutch painter. Mondrian's theories of color and space were the basis of de Stijl's vocabulary, carrying Cubism's abstraction into a new non-figurative dimension. His paintings were reduced to the use of straight lines, squares, rectangles, the primary colors—red, yellow, and blue—and sometimes black and white. Mondrian believed that true reality and perfect harmony could only be obtained through the equilibrium of opposing forces as expressed in the horizontal and the vertical.

Monotype. Trade name for a keyboard-operated typesetting machine that casts characters one at a time from matrices. This machine was invented by Tolbert Lanston in 1897, and was a significant achievement leading to fully automated typesetting. Since its founding, Monotype Corporation has continued as an innovator in the areas of advanced typesetting technology, including state-of-the-art laser equipment; typeface development for books, magazines, and newspapers; typography for business equipment; and the development of typesetting for non-Latin alphabets. U.S. address: 509 W. Golf Road, Arlington Heights, IL 60005.

Stanley Morison (1889–1967). British type designer and advisor. Morison was one of this century's most influential authorities on printing and typography, and a leading revivalist of classical printing types. While typographical advisor to Monotype Corporation in London, his program initiated the design of several original typefaces and revivals of old designs. These include Gill Sans, Perpetua, Rockwell, Ehrhardt, and new versions of Bembo, Baskerville, Garamond, Bell, and Fournier. He is noted for his design of Times New Roman and its far-reaching effect upon printed communication.

Piet Mondrian, *Composition with Blue and Yellow*, 1935.

Max Miedinger. Swiss graphic and type designer. In the late 1950s, Miedinger collaborated with Edouard Hoffman of the Haas type foundry to upgrade the Akzidenz Grotesque fonts. The result of this effort was a typeface called Neue Haas Grotesque. In 1961, this design was produced in Germany by D. Stempel AG and named Helvetica. The simple elegance of Helvetica made it one of the most used typefaces of this century, particularly among designers working in the International Typographic Style. It was first introduced in the United States in the early 1960s.

Modern period. Period of typographic development that took place during the late eighteenth century. Typefaces designed at this time expressed the spirit of the new machine age. They are characterized by flat, unbracketed serifs, extreme contrast between thick-and-thin strokes, and mechanical precision. First designed by Giambattista Bodoni, they have remained popular for nearly two centuries.

Laszlo Moholy-Nagy (1895–1946). American graphic, interior, textile, and exhibition designer, painter, photographer, and filmmaker. Born in Hungary, immigrated to the United States in 1937. Moholy-Nagy's remarkable contribution to design lies not only in his work as a designer, but also in his work as a design educator. He taught at the Bauhaus from 1923 to 1928 and organized and directed the New Bauhaus in Chicago (which eventually became the Institute of Design) from 1937 to 1946. He guided the course of design education with his teaching and writings, and by enlisting great thinkers to aid in a search for a "balance between a biologically sound human existence and the present industrial society." Moholy-Nagy was a Constructivist whose concern for objectivity, geometry, light, space, and kinetics laid a foundation for much of what has happened in design and typography for over fifty years. Significant writings by Moholy-Nagy include *Painting, Photography, Film* (1925), *The New Vision* (1932), and *Vision in Motion* (1947).

Charles W. Morris (1901–1979). American philosopher. The most distinctive contribution of Morris was in the field of semiotics, the general theory of signs. Among design theorists, his approach and vocabulary are widely accepted. He subdivided signs into three parts: syntactics, semantics, and pragmatics. Syntactics is the study of the relations that signs have to each other by virtue of their formal properties; semantics is the study of the relations between signs and what they designate; and pragmatics is the study of the relations between signs and their users. Morris' observations were first recognized in the design world when Laszlo Moholy-Nagy nominated him to professorship at the New Bauhaus in Chicago. His principal writings include *Six Theories of Mind* (1932), *Foundations of the Theory of Signs* (1938), and *Signs, Language, and Behavior* (1946).

Josef Muller-Brockmann (b. 1914). Swiss graphic designer. Muller-Brockmann is the leading theorist and practitioner of objective visual design, and the primary force behind the international Swiss movement. Countless designers have been influenced by his philosophy, which asserts that "graphics should if possible become an anonymous vehicle for the message to be transmitted." He achieves this goal through the use of mathematical grids that establish spatial harmony; and through the reduction of form to clearly stated symbols. Muller-Brockmann's concert and safety posters are the essence of clarity and precision. His writings include *History of Visual Communication* (1971), *History of the Poster* (1971), and *Grid Systems in Graphic Design* (1981).

New Bauhaus. School established by Laszlo Moholy-Nagy in 1937 in Chicago. Faculty included Alexander Archipenko, Gyorgy Kepes and others. Due to financial difficulties, the school closed within one year. It was resurrected however in 1939 as the School of Design and after 1944 as the Institute of Design.

138
139

Robert Rauschenberg
Dam, 1959.

New Graphic Design. Trilingual journal established in 1959 in Zurich. This publication was the voice of the Swiss movement. The ideas of the movement, presented in its articles and by its format, were made known to an international audience. The editors were Josef Muller-Brockmann, Hans Neuberg, Richard P. Lohse, and Carlo Vivarelli.

New York School. Term used to describe a multiplicity of design approaches originating in New York during the 1950s. Designers, drawing upon European influences, evolved an approach to visual problem solving that was uniquely American; it was pragmatic, informal, and highly expressive. Herb Lubalin named it the American School of Graphic Expressionism. Paul Rand, the forerunner of this approach to modern design, was joined by such gifted individuals as Alvin Lustig, Bradbury Thompson, Alex Steinweiss, George Tscherny, Otto Storch, Gene Federico, and Herb Lubalin, to name a few.

Noigandres group. Group formed in 1952 by the three Brazilian poets Haroldo de Campos, Augusto de Campos, and Decio Pignatari. The indefinable name of the group, *Noigandres,* was taken from Ezra Pound's *Cantos,* and was meant to symbolize a new approach to poetry. The formation of the group was significant, for it signaled the beginning of an international movement in concrete poetry. Inspired by the work of Sergei Eisenstein, Futurism, Dada, Stéphane Mallarmé, James Joyce, Ezra Pound, e.e. cummings, and Guillaume Apollinaire, this group freed itself from the restrictions of the "formal rhythmic unit," and became aware "of graphic space as a structural agent" in poetry.

Aldo Novarese (b. 1920). Italian type designer. Over the course of his career, Novarese has designed more than 160 typefaces. Many of these have been for the Turin foundry of Nebiolo, a foundry whose quality he is primarily responsible for. He is the creator of the well-known faces Microgramma and Eurostile, as well as Torino, Nova Augustea, Expert, ITC Symbol, ITC Mixage, and ITC Novarese.

Penrose Annual. Annual publication founded in 1895 in England to record the changes and developments in printing technology. Over the years, the annual has also become a chronicle of the ideas and aesthetics in typography and graphic design.

Photomontage. Technique originating at the beginning of the century that combined several photographs or pieces of photographs into a single composite image. It is thought that Dada artists invented this method as a means to create shocking visual images and chance associations. Raoul Hausmann and Hannah Hoch, both Dada artists from Germany, pioneered this medium. It was later used in the striking political graphics of Rodchenko in Russia, Heartfield in Germany, and in the graphic design of Schuitema and Zwart in Holland.

Photoplastics. Term used by Laszlo Moholy-Nagy to describe his unique method of photomontage. These arrangements, which incorporated images and plastic elements such as line and shape, enabled him to arrive at novel solutions to visual communication problems.

Phototype. Process of setting type by means of photographic projection of letterforms onto film or paper. Prototype had been attempted as early as the late nineteenth century, but did not become a major form of typesetting until the 1960s. Loosened from the restrictive bonds of metal type, designers freely explored the spatial potential and aesthetic nuances of this new technology. The work of Herb Lubalin represents a pioneering effort to define the potential of phototypesetting.

Post-Modernism. Term used to describe the close of the Modern era, and the beginning of a new period in art, design, architecture, and literature. Awareness of changing environmental, social, and technological conditions brought many to the conclusion that the modern aesthetic was not relevant to the late twentieth century. In graphic design, the seeds of Post-Modernism were first sown in Europe with practitioners breaking from the traditions of the International Typographic Style. Objectivity and logic were replaced with intuitive play as designers sought to broaden their visual vocabulary by breaking established rules. Violating grids, creating dynamic spatial fields with disparate elements, employing extreme weight and size contrasts within typographic material, and drawing upon imagery from all periods and cultures are some of the characteristics of this approach.

Ezra Pound (1885–1972). American poet and critic. Many of the foundation stones for the concrete poetry movement were laid by Pound. He is best known for *The Cantos,* an unfinished sequence of ideogrammatic poems that stimulated research by others into the visual nature of words and poetic expression. His work, which may be considered expressionistic, was based upon "field composition," that is, open verse not restricted to traditional patterning.

Print. Bimonthly magazine that presents a broad range of information about visual communication. Intriguing articles about recent trends, profiles of innovative designers, and flashbacks into the history of design each contribute to an editorial potpourri. Each year an annual of regional design is published. Address: 355 Lexington Avenue, New York, NY 10017.

Novum Gebrauchsgraphik. International monthly journal for communication design presented in German, French, English, and Spanish. Developments and trends in areas such as advertising, graphic design, typography, and computer graphics are reported by an international staff of reporters. Regular features appear on designers, illustrators, design education, campaigns, and agencies. Address: Postfach 27, 8000 Muenchen 20, Germany.

Thomas Ockerse. See page 72.

Octavo. International journal of typography published twice per year for a total of four years, 1986–1989. This sixteen-page journal, exquisitely printed and designed, covers a variety of topics. While its focus is primarily on typography within graphic design, it also covers the way in which letterforms are used in the visual arts, poetry, architecture, and the environment. Octavo evolved "from a desire to see an independent publication which acts as a serious forum for the discussion of matters, both contemporary and historical, relating to typographic design."

Mike Parker (b. 1929). American typographer and type director. Born in England. Parker is best known for his work as director of typography at Mergenthaler Linotype. Under his leadership, over 1,000 new typefaces were added to the library, beginning with Helvetica. These include a complete series of Russian, Indian, Arabic, Hebrew, and Greek Scripts, the International Typeface Corporation Library (ITC), licensed versions of designs from other companies, revivals of old designs, and a considerable number of original typefaces from internationally known designers such as Matthew Carter, Adrian Frutiger, and Hermann Zapf. The result was a library that became the standard of the typesetting industry. In 1981 he left Linotype and with Matthew Carter formed Bitstream, Inc., a Cambridge-based digital typefoundry that develops end-user fonts for the desktop publishing market. Parker is currently director of The Company, a typographic consulting service.

Pablo Picasso (1881–1973). Spanish painter and sculptor. Picasso is considered to be the most influential artist of the twentieth century. In 1907, with his painting *Les Demoiselles d'Avignon*, he launched Cubism, a movement that began a revolutionary artistic tradition characterized by abstraction. He fragmented his canvases into simplified shapes that could be viewed simultaneously from different angles. In 1912 he introduced paper collage elements into his work, an approach that became known as Synthetic Cubism. Letterforms and other elements were introduced to signify objects, to create surprising associations, and to establish the reality of painting independent of subject matter.

Charles Sanders Pierce (1839–1914). American philosopher and semiotician. Pierce is the American founder of semiotics. His *Collected Papers* (1931) established an early model for a science of signs, and therefore, an understanding of the complex process of human communication. He defined three classes of signs. These are "icon" (a sign resembling its subject, ie: a photograph of fire is an icon of fire); "index" (a sign pointing to its subject, ie: smoke is an index of fire); and "symbol" (a sign having no inherent relationship to its subject, ie: the word "fire" is a symbol of fire). These designations have aided design theorists in coming to terms with the specific nature of visual messages.

Jacklin Pinsler. See page 76.

Woody Pirtle. See page 80.

Pop art. Movement that originated in the United States and England during the late 1950s and early 1960s. Pop art portrayed all aspects of popular culture. Artists packaged their canvases in comic strips, celebrities, and everyday objects; not as "art" per se, but as a representation of society itself. Leading Pop artists include Andy Warhol, Robert Rauschenberg, Roy Lichtenstein, Jasper Johns, James Rosenquist, Claes Oldenburg, and Richard Hamilton.

Private Press Movement. Revival of the classical principles of book design and typography in small publishing houses and private presses. Beginning just before the turn of the century and continuing to the present, this movement has stressed (to a greater or lesser degree) proportion, harmony, the use of traditional typefaces, symmetrical arrangements of elements on pages, and fine printing. Book-art is a tradition of book design that grew from the private press. Limited edition and "one of" books are created as a medium of artistic expression. While some artists work in a more traditional vein—creating beautifully crafted books with impeccable typography and printing—others redefine the form and function of books by experimenting with new and unusual formats. Individuals such as Bruce Rogers and Frederic Goudy are responsible for this revival. Current practitioners include Jack Stauffacher of the Greenwood Press in California and Walter Hamady of the Perishable Press Ltd. in Wisconsin.

Prouns. See El Lissitzky.

Push Pin Style. See Seymour Chwast and Milton Glaser.

Paul Rand. See page 84.

Robert Rauschenberg (b. 1925). American painter and sculptor. Rauschenberg's "palette" is all of life, and he has led waves of other artists and designers to the same discovery. His singular genius transforms any image, any material, and any idea into something unforgettable. He refuses to be held by any one particular style, yet he is the trailblazer of many new directions—minimal art, conceptual art, Pop art, performance art. In addition to studying with Josef Albers at Black Mountain College in 1949, he has been influenced by other European avant-garde artists. From Kurt Schwitters he acquired an appetite for "junk," to which his marvelous "combines" (large assemblages) will attest; and from Duchamp he assimilated a desire to engage the absurd.

Renaissance. See Classicism.

Paul Renner (1878–1956). German graphic and type designer. From 1927 to 1930, Renner designed Futura, a typeface that best represented the ambience of "the new typography." It originally consisted of fifteen alphabets (including two display faces) geometrically constructed in a wide range of sizes and weights. Because of its elemental character, Futura has enjoyed steady popularity since first being introduced by the Bauer foundry.

Gerrit Rietveld (1888–1964). Dutch architect and furniture designer. The furniture of Rietveld ranks among the most significant artistic achievements of this century. He created about seventy-five objects, three of which guided the theoretical development of de Stijl: the Red/blue chair (1918), the Berlin chair (1923), and the end table (1923). The Red/blue chair justified a neoplasticist belief that the use of reduced form and color could result in the creation of worthy artifacts. Rietveld's Schroder house, designed and built in Utrecht in 1923, represents his reductivist theories applied to architecture. Theodore Brown describes the house as "a group of freely related planes and lines that appear to hover in space."

Alexander Rodchenko (1891–1956). Russian painter, sculptor, graphic designer, architect, and photographer. Rodchenko was a Constructivist dedicated to social reform through art. Unlike Kandinsky and Malevich who sought the mystical in their painting, Rodchenko wanted only to unveil the reality of contemporary society. His commitment to the leftist principles of art and life in revolutionary Russia were embedded within his powerful political graphics. He used photomontage forcefully, combining it with simple but bold sans serif letters that screamed a renunciation of the past and asserted the faith of the present. Examples of his finest work are designs for the journal *LEF* ("Left front of the Arts"), and his political and film posters.

Emil Ruder (1914–1970). Swiss graphic designer and educator. In 1942, Ruder began his career as a design educator at the Allgemeine Kunstgewerbeschule in Basel, where he headed the typography classes. In 1965, he became director of the school, a position he held until his death. Ruder imparted his philosophy vicariously to students throughout the world with his classic text *Typographie* (1967). A preface to the book reads: "Contemporary typography is not based primarily on the flash of inspiration and striking idea. It is based on a grasp of the essential underlying laws of form, on thinking in connected wholes, so that it avoids on the one hand turgid rigidity and monotony and on the other unmotivated arbitrary interpretations."

Mike Salisbury (b. 1941). American graphic designer. During the 1960s, a changing editorial climate forced designers to re-examine the role of the magazine and to seek new ways of communicating with this medium. Salisbury—partly inspired by Pop art—infused within his magazines the artifacts of popular culture. With his redesign of *Rolling Stone* in 1974, each article received a different typographic treatment consisting of several wildly contrasting typefaces. This uninhibited approach to magazine typography was soon seen in magazines across the country.

George Salter (1897–1967). Graphic and book designer, calligrapher, and illustrator. Born in Germany, immigrated to the United States in 1934. Salter has been called "America's Edward Johnston," for throughout his career he contributed to a revived interest in the art of calligraphy. He was a leader in the development of American book jacket design as well, having served as a designer to several major publishing houses during his career. Of these, he is best remembered for the jackets he designed for Alfred A. Knopf, and his covers for Mercury Publications. Salter most often employed hand lettering and illustration for his jacket designs, believing that this was the best way to accurately represent the allusive nature of books. In his designs of the 1930s, he popularized the use of the airbrush to achieve modulations of form.

Kurt Schwitters, pages from *Merz II* devoted to typography in advertising, 1924.

Alexander Rodchenko poster for "Kino Glaz," 1924.

Bruce Rogers (1870–1957). American book and type designer. Rogers was an influential book designer active until the 1950s who worked for some of the most important printing houses in America. Among these was the Riverside Press in Cambridge, Massachusetts, where he designed a number of books strongly oriented in the Arts and Crafts tradition. His books met the demands of modern production methods while also maintaining aesthetic beauty. During his career he designed about 700 books, turning to a number of inspired sources including the works of Nicolas Jenson and the French Renaissance. Centaur, his typeface design of 1916, is an adaptation of Jenson's roman in the Eusebius of 1470. It is one of the finest American type designs ever produced.

Edward Rondthaler (b. 1905). American typographer and inventor. Rondthaler led technical advances in phototypesetting processes that altered the course of American typographic design. He participated in the development of the Rutherford Photolettering Machine, and in 1936 headed Photolettering, a firm that made phototype commercially available for the first time. In 1970, he joined Herb Lubalin and Aaron Burns to establish the International Typeface Corporation.

Diter Rot (b. 1930). German poet, painter, sculptor, filmmaker, furniture and graphic designer. Rot is best known for his concrete poetry and experimental books of the 1950s and 1960s. During this time he was acquainted with Eugen Gomringer in Switzerland and maintained close contact with the "Darmstadt Circle," an influential group of concrete poets in Germany (Emmett Williams, an American poet, was a member of this group). From his remote private press in Iceland, using his remarkable knowledge of typographic material, he produced typographic ideograms that can be freely interpreted by readers, and books that may be experienced as plastic entities approached from any direction. Throughout his life, Rot's work has represented the antithesis of convention; novel ways of looking at the world have evolved into projects such as his collaborative Newspaper for Everyone, and the Family Publishing House.

Willem Sandberg (1897–1984). Dutch graphic and exhibition designer. While in hiding during World War II Sandberg produced *experimenta typographica*, a series of eighteen experiments that influenced much of his later work. He was appointed director of the Stedelijk Museum in 1945, and in the same year presented a retrospective exhibition on the work of Henryk Werkman, a Dutch printer/painter from Groningen who was shot by the Germans just days before the liberation of Groningen. Sandberg's use of bold typography can be traced to Werkman's influence. Exhibitions, catalogs, and other materials designed by Sandberg for the museum had a far-reaching effect upon museum publications throughout Europe and America.

Paula Scher. See page 88.

Paul Schuitema (1897–1973). Dutch graphic and exhibition designer, painter, photographer, and filmmaker. Schuitema's work, like that of Piet Zwart, represents a Dutch brand of the "new typography." He combined photography and photomontage with rather unrefined sans serif type, placed at angles on the page to imply movement. His color palette consisted primarily of black and red. Some of his best work was done for the Berkel company, and includes booklets, advertisements, and exhibitions. The essence of Schuitema's approach is documented in his book *New Typographical Design in 1930* (1961).

Kurt Schwitters (1887–1948). German poet, artist, and graphic designer. Schwitters created a one-man movement, a branch of Dada, called *Merz*. In 1919 he completed his first *Merz* composition, a collage made "with the help of nails and glue, paper and rags, hammers and oil, paint, parts of machinery, and bits of lace." These were highly refined juxtapositions of form, color, and texture. From 1923 to 1932 Schwitters published the periodical *Merz*, featuring contributions of many of the leading avant-garde artists throughout Europe. Even though the Cubists and the Futurists had already explored the use of found materials in their paintings, it is Schwitters who is remembered most for revealing the communicative power of ordinary objects.

S

Sumner Stone, Stone family, 1987.

Typographic arrangement by Min Wang.

R. D. Scudellari. See page 92.

Seybold Report on Publishing Systems. Thoroughly analyzes developments in text editing, type-setting, and composition hardware and soft-ware and other front-end (pre-press) systems for newspaper, commercial, and in-plant applications. Address: Seybold Publications, Inc., Box 644, Media, PA 19063.

Semiotics. Science that studies all aspects of human communicative behavior. Its origins can be traced as far back as Plato, but it was only at the beginning of the twentieth century with the writings of Charles Sanders Pierce and Ferdinand de Saussure that it became a con-crete area of study. Semiotics involves the analysis of language, which is a system of in-teracting signs that express ideas. De Saus-sure was the first to recognize that "a science that studies the life of signs is conceivable," and indeed, the field has grown to include natural languages, written languages, visual communication, mass communication, rhetoric, anthropology, psychology, and biology.

Society of Typographic Arts (STA). National organi-zation founded in 1927. The STA provides professional and social resources, and educa-tional programs for the design community. Activities include conferences, seminars, workshops, and exhibitions. The aim of the organization is to promote design and typo-graphic excellence for the benefit of the entire society. Address: 233 East Ontario, Suite 301, Chicago, IL 60611.

Ardengo Soffici (1879–1964). Italian painter and writer. Of the Futurists involved with both painting and poetry, Soffici was one of the most inno-vative. He created many fine "free-word" poems, in which the typography expressed the emotional content of the text. "No longer a mute symbol of convention," he said, "but a live form amongst live forms, the letter becomes one with the material of the repre-sentation." In 1913 with Giovanni Papini, he edited *Lacerba,* the journal that launched the Futurist revolution against classical typogra-phy. Its pages included a range of philosophy, literature, and social criticism.

Jack W. Stauffacher (b. 1920). American book designer and typographer. Stauffacher has worked as a book typographer since 1935. He founded the Greenwood Press in San Francisco in 1947 and has since been an important influence upon the American private press movement. His work, which is classically oriented, is concerned with the aesthetics of typography and the integration of historical type styles. In 1979 he founded the Center for Typographic Language in San Francisco. He is the author of *A Printed Word Has Its Own Measure* (1969), and through the Greenwood Press has written, edited, and published many works, including *Janson: A Definitive Collection* (1954), and *A Search for the Typographic Form of Plato's Phaedrus* (1978).

Gertrude Stein (1874–1946). American writer. Stein applied to literature what Mondrian had dis-covered in art: the expression of pure reality. She believed that words should be "arranged in a system to pointing," and that linguistic structures should be employed that represent things as they are; thus her motto, "A rose is a rose is a rose." During her expatriate life in France she developed a re-petitive, non-associational style. She is best known for *The Autobiography of Alice B. Toklas* (1933).

Sumner Stone (b. 1945). American type designer. Trained as a calligrapher and as a mathematician, Stone was type director at Autologic and Ca-mex. Upon becoming type director of Adobe Systems he designed the first original type family, named Stone, for the page-description language PostScript. The extended Stone family consists of eighteen typefaces including serif, sans serif, and informal.

Otto Storch (b. 1913). American graphic designer. Storch studied under Alexey Brodovitch, acquiring the master's affinity for photography and typography. He is known for his ability to create surprising and poetic messages through the formal relationships of type and image. During the 1950s and 1960s, as art director of *McCall's,* he contributed to the growth in visual sophistication of American magazines.

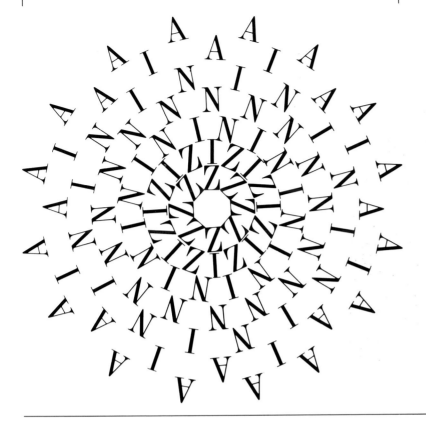

Mary Ellen Solt, *Zinnia*, 1965. Typography by John Dearstyne.

Mary Ellen Solt (b. 1920). American concrete poet and educator. In 1968, Solt published *Concrete Poetry: A World View*, the first comprehensive survey of the international movement of concrete poetry. The book includes a thorough introduction that traces the history of the movement and discusses the work of significant poets. Over the years, it has done more to advance theories of the new literature than any other source. During her formative years, Solt was influenced considerably by Ian Hamilton Finlay of Scotland, with whom she kept close contact. Her poetry includes *Moonshot Sonnet* (1964), and *Forsythia* (1966).

Herbert Spencer (b. 1924). British graphic designer and educator. Spencer's principal contribution outside of Britain consists of his writings. Two of his books, *The Visible Word* (1969), a source that covers the subject of legibility, and *Pioneers of Modern Typography* (1969), a short history of the modern movement, have been read widely throughout the United States and Europe. He was also the editor of *Typographica* (1949–1967), a magazine that served as an international voice on typography, and the *Penrose Annual*. In 1987 he edited *The Liberated Page*, an anthology of the major typographic experiments of this century as recorded in *Typographica* magazine.

Anton Stankowski (b. 1906). German graphic designer and painter. Stankowski is noted for his ability to communicate invisible processes—such as telecommunications and computer technology—through the use of abstract form. His knowledge of form language has been strengthened over the years by a theoretical dialogue established between his fine and applied art. Other factors have also contributed to his unique vision. While living in Zurich between 1929 and 1937, he was closely associated with the major Swiss designers, including Max Bill and Herbert Matter, who nurtured his mastery of Constructivist design and concrete art. Stankowski is also known for his darkroom experiments of form and texture.

Structuralism. Approach to thinking about the world that recognizes relationships rather than independently existing phenomena. Terrence Hawkes elaborates: "At its simplest, it claims that the nature of every element in any given situation has no significance by itself, and in fact is determined by its relationship to all the other elements involved in that situation." Structuralism is closely related to semiotics, for it is upon the structural relationships of signs that signification is based. It is an approach used in many areas, including psychology, anthropology, literature, and visual communication.

Louis Sullivan (1856–1924). American architect. Sullivan's experimental use of steel frames in architecture established him as an early prophet of the structural grid and of Modernism. And although his buildings were clothed with a non-obtrusive Art Nouveau ornament, he was one of the first to speculate about a new style of unadorned architecture. In his book *Ornament in Architecture* (1892), Sullivan stated that "it would be greatly for our aesthetic good, if we should refrain from using ornament for a period of years...." Architects such as Adolf Loos translated these words into buildings of radical simplicity and purity, and Sullivan's words, "form follows function," became a principal slogan of the twentieth century.

Suprematism. See Kasimir Malevich.

Surrealism. Movement in art and literature founded by the French poet André Breton in Paris in 1924. The surrealists affirmed that the dream world of the unconscious mind as explored by Freud is more real than the world of the senses. The aim of the movement, according to Breton, was to combine both worlds into a "superreality." This would be achieved by rejecting artistic, social, and moral conventions, and by freeing the senses to explore the hidden truths of the unconscious mind. In the beginning the movement was dominated by writers, including Tristan Tzara, Louis Aragon, and Paul Eluard who stirred the unconscious with illogical and startling word plays. The first Surrealist painter was Giorgio de Chirico, followed by Max Ernst, René Magritte, and Salvador Dali.

144
145

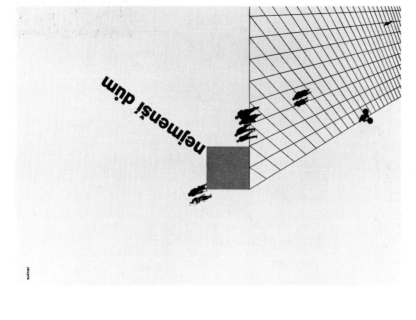

Ladislav Sutnar, jacket design
for *Nejmensi dum* (Minimum Housing), 1931.

Ladislav Sutnar (1897–1969). American graphic and exhibition designer. Born in Czechoslovakia, immigrated to the United States in 1939. Sutnar is America's articulate proponent of the "new typography," and "information design." He is known for his ability to use dynamic form as a means to bring cohesiveness and order to complex information. In his book *Visual Design in Action* (1961) he states: "Depending upon the requirements of specific problem needs, the varied aspects of design can be reduced to three interacting, fundamental principles—function, flow, and form." Sutnar's use of new forms that extend "beyond the field of familiar symbols" is demonstrated in work such as Sweet's industrial catalogs and identity systems for Addox Business Machines.

Swiss typography. See International Typographic Style.

Bradbury Thompson. See page 96.

Transitional period. Period of typographic development that took place during the eighteenth century (c. 1720–1780). This was a time of typographic evolution when designers gradually increased the contrast between thick-and-thin strokes, sharpened and straightened the serifs, and increased the vertical stress of rounded letterforms. The type designs of John Baskerville, Fournier, Martin, Austin, and Bell represent the midpoint between Old Style and Modern typefaces.

Georg Trump (1896–1985). German type and book designer, and educator. Trump spent most of his professional career as a teacher of lettering and typography, but also devoted himself to the design of typefaces, which include a range of scripts, romans, Egyptians, and a sans serif. His educational career included a 1928 appointment with the Meisterschule fur Deutschlands Buchdrucker (advanced school of book printing). Paul Renner was head of the school at the time and the young and radical Jan Tschichold was a teacher at the institution. Characteristic of Trump's types is a calligraphic liveliness and skilled precision. His designs, which include Schadow, City, Delphin, Amati, Codex, Trump Mediaeval, and Mauritius became very popular in the United States during the last years of his life.

Type Directors Club (TDC). New York–based organization whose goals are to raise typographic standards throughout the industry, to disseminate information about typography and related materials, and to work cooperatively with other organizations having similar aims. Since its founding in 1946, the organization has sponsored monthly luncheon lectures. Competitions and exhibitions encourage excellence among designers throughout the world. Address: 60 East 42nd Street, Suite 1130, New York, NY 10165.

TypeWorld. Biweekly newspaper for the electronic publishing industry. This tabloid is the best source for up-to-the-minute information on industry developments. Company news, product descriptions, hardware and software advancements, typographical improvements, and announcements about seminars and conferences are some of the issues covered. Address: P.O. Box 170, 35 Pelham Road, Salem, NH 03079.

Typografische Monatsblaetter. Bimonthly Swiss periodical presented in English, French, and German that reviews individuals, projects, and ideas related to the field of typography. Address: Zollikoser AG, Fuerstenland Str. 122, CH–9001, St. Gallen, Switzerland.

Typogram. Letterforms combined into visual configurations that communicate brief, memorable, and instantaneously perceived messages. Often used as logotypes for mastheads or symbols for visual identification, typograms were actively explored as a by-product of display photographic typesetting.

Typographica. Magazine published and distributed internationally by Lund Humphries. During its seventeen years of existence (1949–1967), *Typographica* functioned as a catalyst for new ideas, and profoundly influenced the theory and practice of typography throughout the world. Articles explored historical as well as contemporary issues.

146
147

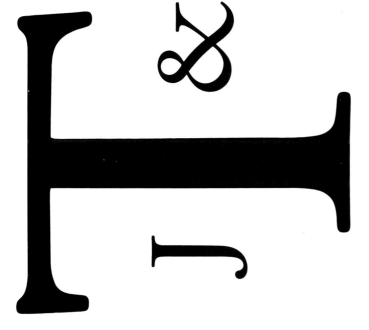

Sabon

Jan Tschichold

1964

George Tscherny (b. 1924). American graphic designer. Born in Hungary, immigrated to the United States in 1941. Over the years, Tscherny has developed a personal approach to design that is uniquely American; he never has and he never will recycle old form or follow a formula. He speaks revealingly about his attitudes in the 1950s and 1960s: "I had my differences with many of my colleagues during those years: their fascination with man-made, ersatz materials, the sterile 'one-typeface' ideology of some, and the typographic gluttony of others." Tscherny's design and typography solutions, which emerge from the substance of problems, exhibit drama, surprise, and economy of means. His many corporate clients have included the W. R. Grace Company, IBM, RCA, Rockwell International, and Air Canada.

Jan Tschichold (1902–1974). Swiss graphic and type designer. Tschichold was the guiding force behind the "new typography." His authoritative theories were discussed as early as 1925 with the manifesto "Elementare Typographie," and in 1928 with *Die Neue Typographie*. Within the self-restricted boundaries of functionalism, he paid attention to the smallest of details and continually developed the tenets of the movement. The same zeal surrounding his conversion to modernism accompanied his departure from it. In the late 1930s he reverted to classical typography, citing as reasons the similarities between the absolutism of the "new typography" and the totalitarianism of National Socialism, and the inability to meet the complexities of the earlier approach to meet the complexities of book design. Most of his later work was in book design, Penguin being his most notable client. In 1966 he designed Sabon, a typeface intended to be set on Linotype and Monotype equipment, by hand as foundry type, or as phototype without a perceptible difference in the characters.

Typomundus 20. First international exhibition of typography. The exhibition, which was sponsored by the now defunct International Center for the Typographic Arts (ICTA), took place in 1965. Its purpose was to gather, preserve, and document the significant typography of the twentieth century. Ten thousand entries were judged by twelve world-renowned designers. These were Max Caflisch (Switzerland), Carl Dair (Canada), Louis Dorfsman (United States), Olle Eksell (Sweden), Roger Excoffon (France), Hiromu Hara (Japan), Oldrich Hlavsa (Czechoslovakia), Hans Neuberg (Switzerland), Anton Stankowski (Germany), Horst Erich Wolter (Germany), Hermann Zapf (Germany), and Piet Zwart (Netherlands). A catalog, *Typomundus 20*, was published by Reinhold Publishing Corporation in 1966.

Typophoto. Term used by Laszlo Moholy-Nagy to describe the integration of typography and photography into "a new visual literature." "Photography," he said, "is highly effective when used as typographical material. It may appear as illustration beside the words, or in the form of 'phototext' in place of words, as a precise form of representation so objective as to permit no individual interpretation."

Tristan Tzara (1896–1963). Romanian poet. Tzara was a fiery and uninhibited intellectual who with Hugo Ball initiated Dada in Zurich in 1916. "What would Dada have been," said Hans Richter, "without Tzara's poems, his insatiable ambition, his manifestos, not to speak of the riots he produced in such masterly fashion?" His exploration of chance, nonsense, and simultaneous poetry was indispensible to the movement, as was his editorship of the periodical *Dada*, which he also designed. The free use of typography, in which jumbled typefaces activated the page, carried the messages of the Zurich Dadaists to many parts of Europe.

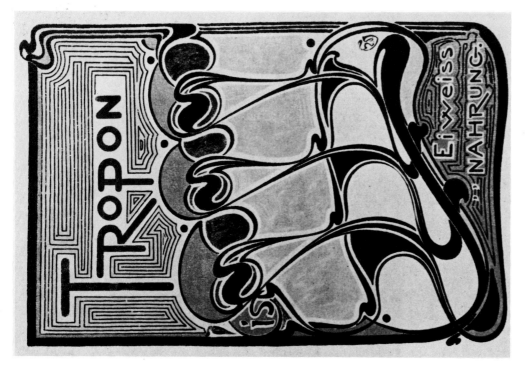

Henri van de Velde, poster for a food concentrate company, 1899.

U&lc. Quarterly tabloid published by the International Typeface Corporation. *U&lc* is primarily intended as a showcase for ITC's library of typefaces, but also contains regular features on typographic technology, history, satiric art, and significant designers. Advertisements from various manufacturers and suppliers of typographic materials are helpful resources as well. Address: 2 Hammarskjold Plaza, New York, NY 10017.

Ulm: Journal of the Ulm School for Design. Publication that documented the achievements of the Ulm School for Design in the fields of education and research. It also discussed unanswered questions of design philosophy, method, and teaching. *Ulm 21,* the last issue, was published in 1968 signalling the closing of the school itself. This valuable resource is available at libraries for research and study.

Daniel Berkely Updike (1860–1941). American book designer and historian. Updike's two-volume study, *Printing Types, Their History, Form and Use* (1937), is an in-depth resource on the early history and development of typography and printing. In addition to this important contribution, he is known for the design and printing of fine books—in the tradition of William Morris—at the Merrymount Press near Boston.

Henri van de Velde (1863–1957). Belgian architect, painter, graphic designer, and educator. Van de Velde combined aspects of Art Nouveau and the English Arts and Crafts Movement into a cohesive style reflecting the emerging modern era. He believed that ornament was capable of symbolic expression, and that it should arise "by means of pure structure." In other words, it should be a logical extension of construction rather than added as surface decoration. Ornament in his book designs evolved from figurative motifs to abstract, expressive forms. Van de Velde reorganized the Weimar Academy of Fine Arts and the Weimar Arts and Crafts Institute into a combined school that later became known as the Staatliches Bauhaus. He nominated Walter Gropius as head of the school.

Mies van der Rohe (1889–1969). American architect, furniture designer, and educator. Born in Germany, immigrated to the United States in

Robert Venturi (b. 1925). American architect. During the 1960s, a few rebellious architects began to soften the hard edges of modern architecture. The most significant and controversial of these was Venturi. In his book, *Learning from Las Vegas,* he recognized the need for social and environmental responsibility in an age of dwindling resources. He approached architecture as part of an urban communication environment, and was one of the first to employ supergraphics and ornamentation as information vehicles.

Victoriana. Everyday objects produced during the reign of England's Queen Victoria between 1837 and 1901. This was a period of economic and industrial development where new techniques in mass production made household objects cheaper and more widely available. Because middle class patrons lacked a foundation of art appreciation, they found pleasure in objects that were bright, gaudy, unrefined, and overly ornamental. In the twentieth century Victoriana found popularity among collectors, for what was once considered to be in bad taste achieved an innocent charm. Contemporary graphic designers have used this endless supply of objects, advertisements, engravings, and letterforms as a resource in solving visual problems.

Vienna Secession. Style of decorative art founded in Austria in 1897 that rejected the floral Art Nouveau of France and Germany for an approach characterized by the use of clean, curvilinear sans serif lettering; rhythmic fields of contrasting geometric patterns consisting of circles, squares, triangles, and other simple shapes; and orderly compositions. Leaders of the group included its guiding spirit, Gustav Klimt; the architects J. J. Olbrich and Josef Hoffmann; Koloman Moser, Alfred Roller, Berthold Loffler, and Rudolf Von Larisch. *Ver Sacrum* (1898–1903), one of the most striking publications at the turn of the century, enabled these artists to test their ideas.

Massimo Vignelli. See page 100.

Theo van Doesburg, cover design
of the third issue of *Mechano*, 1922.

Visible Language. Quarterly journal concerned with the unique role and properties of written language. Scholarly articles explore a wide range of historical, theoretical, and pragmatic issues. Address: Wayne State University Press, Leonard N. Simons Building, 5959 Woodward Avenue, Detroit, MI 48202.

Rudolf Von Larisch (1856–1934). German calligrapher, type designer, and educator. Von Larisch was a reformer of late nineteenth-century calligraphy and a pioneer of new approaches in the art of lettering. As a teacher in the Vienna School of Art, he encouraged students to work in many materials, to express their individuality, and to become adept in many different kinds of lettering activity—from stone carving to type design and punchcutting. This attitude became prevalent throughout Germany and other areas, leading artists and designers to an interest in the relationship between calligraphy and type design—an interest that continues to this day.

Beatrice Warde (1900–1969). American writer, editor, typographic scholar, and typographer. Warde is remembered more for her research, articles, and lectures about typography than for her ability as a typographer. She began her career with American Typefounders Company in New Jersey as an assistant librarian, and it was here that she developed a foundation of knowledge that would establish her as a leading authority on typography. In 1925, Stanley Morison (typographic advisor to Monotype Corporation) invited Beatrice and her husband, Frederic Warde, an accomplished type designer, to assist him in England on a number of projects. (During a visit to the United States that same year, Morison had met Beatrice and the two of them became quite smitten with each other. After moving to England, the Wardes' relationship ended, and a lifelong companionship and collaboration ensued between Beatrice and Stanley.) Beatrice became Director of Publicity for the British Monotype Corporation in 1929, and she remained in England until her death. Among her many writings is a significant article entitled "The Garamond Types," published in 1926 in Number 5 of *The Fleuron*, under her pseudonym Paul Beaujon.

1938. As an early exponent of the "new architecture," van der Rohe is important for introducing a machine aesthetic—simple geometric form stripped of ornament—that grew from the unification of modern materials and engineering technology. Steel and glass skyscraper experiments of the 1920s exemplified this aesthetic and foreshadowed such projects as the Barcelona pavilion (1929), the Tugendhat House (1930), Crown Hall at the Illinois Institute of Technology (1955–1956), and the Seagram Building in New York (1956–1959). His furniture designs include the famous Barcelona chair (1927). Van der Rohe was appointed director of the Bauhaus in 1930 and remained until its closing in 1933. After coming to America, he continued architectural practice and became head of the architecture department at the Illinois Institute of Technology.

Theo van Doesburg (1883–1931). Dutch architect, painter, sculptor, graphic designer, and writer. In 1917, van Doesburg founded de Stijl, and throughout his career remained active in spreading its theories. From 1917 until his death in 1931, he designed and published the journal *de Stijl*. A special issue of this publication entitled *Anthology-Bonset* (1921) contains a collection of his Dadaist poems. These poems feature typography that becomes an integral part of the message through variations of size, weight, and typeface. Van Doesburg was closely associated with the Bauhaus, and from 1921 to 1923 he conducted lectures that were primarily attended by students of the school.

Jan van Krimpen (1892–1958). Dutch type and book designer. Van Krimpen spent most of his career with the important printing firm Enschede en Zonen in Haarlem. His work is characterized by an austere clarity of form resulting from a highly personal vision. Although he studied calligraphy his type designs are rather non-calligraphic; he saw the two disciplines as being unrelated. Rather than merely copying old typefaces, van Krimpen reinterpreted them and attempted to extend typographic traditions. Lutetia, Romanee, Romulus, and Spectrum comprise a sampling of his type designs.

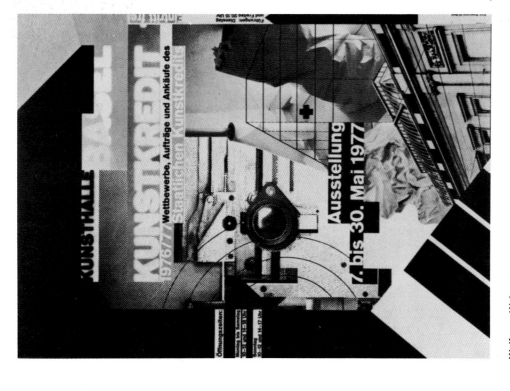

Wolfgang Weingart
poster for an exhibition, 1978.

Andy Warhol (1930–1987). American pop artist and filmmaker. Warhol became known during the 1960s for his mechanical reproductions of everyday objects such as soup cans and portraits of celebrities. He attempted to show through coarse, indifferent, and repetitive work that art and mass culture are one and the same. His films, which explored controversial aspects of feeling and behavior, include *The Chelsea Girls* (1966).

Debra Weier. See page 104.

Wolfgang Weingart (b. 1941). Swiss graphic designer. Weingart is a largely self-taught designer (he was trained as a compositor) who since 1968 has taught typography at the Allgemeine Kunstgewerbeschule in Basel. Rather than continuing in the established Swiss doctrines, he explored new directions that alluded to Post-Modernism and influenced typographic education throughout the world. Wide letter-spacing, the use of contrasting sizes and weights of letterforms, new devices to direct readers through information, and the layering of complex information textures using film positives are among his innovations. For Weingart, everything is capable of performing typographically. His "morphological typecase," for instance, includes repetitive typography, outer-space typography, typewriter typography, listing typography, and middle-axis typography.

Emil Rudolf Weiss (1875–1942). German poet, painter, and type designer. Weiss was one of the early leaders of German typography, along with Rudolf Koch and Otto Eckmann. He became interested in type design through writing, eventually producing a number of faces bearing his name, Weiss Antiqua among them. These became popular in the United States through the Bauer type foundry.

Henryk Werkman (1882–1945). Dutch printer, painter, and graphic designer. In an isolated northern Dutch town called Groningen, Werkman worked as a jobbing printer while painting and printing experimental typographic compositions called *druksels* in his spare time. These prints were made by organizing odd pieces of wood type and typographic rules into simple compositions and printing them with a hand press onto coarse paper. In 1923

Berthold Wolpe (b. 1905). German type designer. In 1924, Wolpe studied with Rudolf Koch at the Offenbach Technical Institute. Here he learned metal work and lettering and became involved in many collaborative projects with Koch. His types reflect a superior sense of formal articulation and sturdy individualism. He designed several popular faces—Albertus, Trajanus, and Pegasus among them.

Woodtype. Handset display type prevalent during the nineteenth and early twentieth centuries. It was created due to the need for large type in advertising, and made possible by the invention of the lateral router by Darius Wells in 1827. These decorative and novelty faces had been rejected for many years due to the influence of the Modern movement. In the 1950s and 1960s, however, designers seeking a more expressive typographic approach were lured by the charm and personality of Victorian faces. This marked the beginning of a woodtype revival and the eventual conversion of hundreds of earlier designs to film. The revival was spurred by Rob Roy Kelly's *American Wood Types* (1969), and the Morgan Press collection of Victorian faces.

Frank Lloyd Wright (1867–1959). American architect, furniture and graphic designer. Wright's career began in Louis Sullivan's Chicago office and progressed through several phases; he remains America's most astute romantic. At the turn of the century he was at the forefront of Modernism, working in the Prairie School of domestic architecture. His houses, which were influenced by Japanese architecture, were low and long with strip windows and overhanging eaves. His concern was not in making pretty facades, but in creating ethereal spaces in which people could live and work. Projects in his later career ranged from neo-Victorian extravagances to the streamlined Expressionism of the Guggenheim Museum (1946–1956). From time to time, Wright also turned his attention to graphic design, fabrics, wallpapers, stained glass, lettering, and book design.

150
151

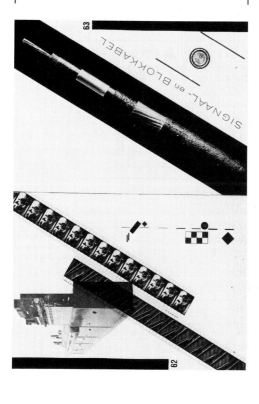

Piet Zwart, spread from the N. V. Nederlandsche Kabelfabriek Catalogue, 1928.

Hermann Zapf, drawings and alphabets of Marconi Roman, 1974.

he began the printing and production of a small magazine entitled *The Next Call*, which was distributed to a limited number of people worldwide. Werkman's unique use of materials and vivid typographic compositions were a major contribution to modern typography. He was executed by the Nazis in 1945.

Emmett Williams (b. 1925). American concrete poet. As an expatriate American living in Europe, Williams was one of the most original poets connected with the international concrete poetry movement. He found freedom in the material substance of language, for this dimension possessed qualities with unlimited communicative potential. He became a master of permutational poems, able to achieve unexpected meanings through the systematic employment of signs. This is demonstrated in his kinetic book *Sweethearts*, one of the most important achievements in concrete poetry. He was a member of the Darmstadt Circle of concrete poets in Germany, which included Daniel Spoerri and Claus Bremer, and was closely associated with Diter Rot.

Dietmar Winkler. See page 108.

Henry Wolf (b. 1925). American graphic designer, photographer, and painter. Born in Austria, immigrated to the United States in 1941. Wolf is an extraordinary problem solver, in command of all facets of visual language. Having studied under Alexey Brodovitch at the New School for Social Research during the late 1940s, he began his career on firm visual footing. He inherited Brodovitch's love for beautiful typography and his eye for provocative photography, but carried these attributes to new heights. As art director of *Esquire*, *Harper's Bazaar*, and *Show* magazines, he created dream-like covers and sophisticated interiors that masterfully welded form to content.

Carl Zahn (b. 1928). American graphic designer. Zahn is a designer of amazing versatility, who since 1956 has served as a graphic designer at the Boston Museum of Fine Arts. He is concerned with presenting information clearly through typographic refinement and with exploring typography as an inexhaustible source of visual stimulation. His work, which has been influential in setting standards for museum publication design throughout the United States, was recognized in the American Institute of Graphic Art's "Fifty Best Books of the Year" exhibition for several consecutive years. William Seitz's book about Zahn, *Carl Zahn*, was published by Brandeis University in 1969.

Hermann Zapf (b. 1918). German type and book designer, and calligrapher. Zapf has created more than 250 type designs throughout his brilliant career, but his importance is not so much connected to the quantity of his work as with the quality of his approach. His designs reflect an understanding and appreciation of the typographical past as well as a commitment to present cultural contexts. Two of his most popular Roman faces—Palatino and Optima—combine the lively variations of calligraphic letters with the geometrical precision and simplicity of the modern age. Zapf's type designs possess the qualities of writing, a fact that comes as no surprise, for he is a master calligrapher whose spiritual teacher was Rudolf Koch.

Piet Zwart (1885–1977). Dutch interior, industrial, and graphic designer, and photographer. Zwart synthesized ideas of de Stijl and Dadaism into a charged typography that presented information clearly and imaginatively by means of vigorous contrasts and fields of typographical tension. He began his career in 1919 as an architect and interior designer working first in the office of Jan Wils, who was a member of de Stijl; and in 1923 for H. P. Berlage. But by 1925, most of his time was devoted to typography. His work for the Nederlandse Kabelfabriek in Delft is characteristic of his fluid collage technique and represents some of his finest work. Zwart referred to himself as a *typotekt*, a term analogous to his method of constructing typographic designs.

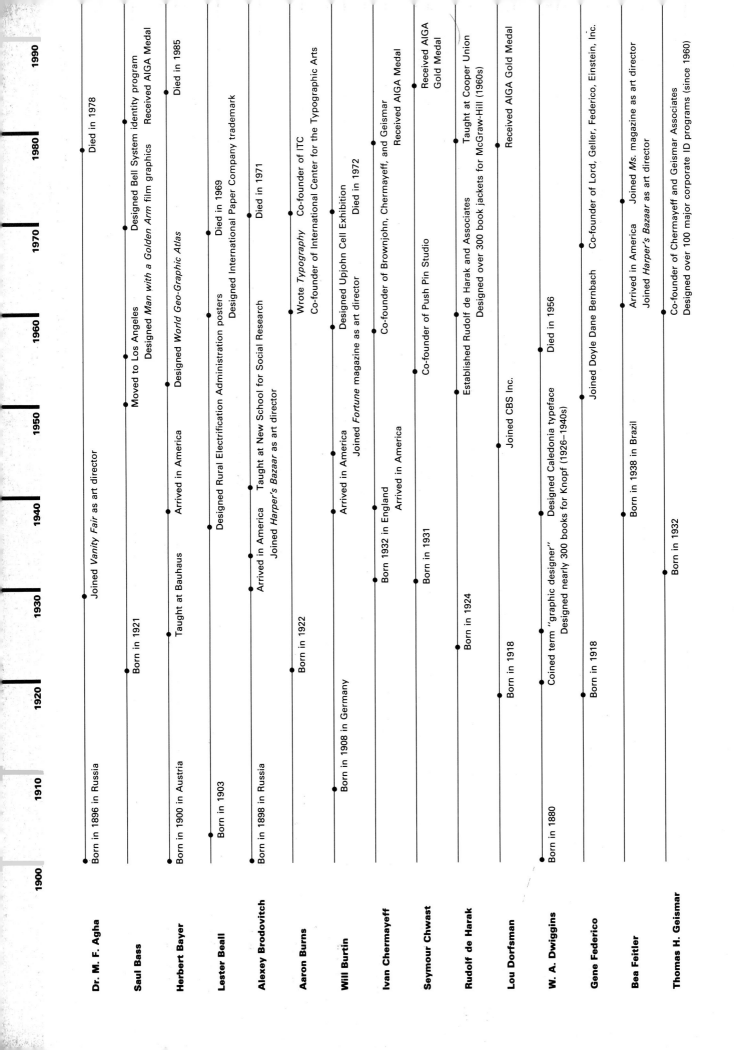

Timeline scale: 1900 · 1910 · 1920 · 1930 · 1940 · 1950 · 1960 · 1970 · 1980 · 1990

Dr. M. F. Agha
Born in 1896 in Russia · Joined *Vanity Fair* as art director · Died in 1978

Saul Bass
Born in 1921 · Moved to Los Angeles · Designed *Man with a Golden Arm* film graphics · Designed Bell System identity program · Received AIGA Medal

Herbert Bayer
Born in 1900 in Austria · Taught at Bauhaus · Arrived in America · Designed *World Geo-Graphic Atlas* · Died in 1985

Lester Beall
Born in 1903 · Designed Rural Electrification Administration posters · Died in 1969 · Designed International Paper Company trademark

Alexey Brodovitch
Born in 1898 in Russia · Arrived in America · Taught at New School for Social Research · Joined *Harper's Bazaar* as art director · Died in 1971

Aaron Burns
Born in 1922 · Wrote *Typography* · Co-founder of ITC · Co-founder of International Center for the Typographic Arts

Will Burtin
Born in 1908 in Germany · Arrived in America · Joined *Fortune* magazine as art director · Designed Upjohn Cell Exhibition · Died in 1972

Ivan Chermayeff
Born 1932 in England · Arrived in America · Co-founder of Brownjohn, Chermayeff, and Geismar · Received AIGA Medal

Seymour Chwast
Born in 1931 · Co-founder of Push Pin Studio · Received AIGA Gold Medal

Rudolf de Harak
Born in 1924 · Established Rudolf de Harak and Associates · Designed over 300 book jackets for McGraw-Hill (1960s) · Taught at Cooper Union

Lou Dorfsman
Born in 1918 · Joined CBS Inc. · Received AIGA Gold Medal

W. A. Dwiggins
Born in 1880 · Coined term "graphic designer" · Designed Caledonia typeface · Designed nearly 300 books for Knopf (1926–1940s) · Died in 1956

Gene Federico
Born in 1918 · Joined Doyle Dane Bernbach · Co-founder of Lord, Geller, Federico, Einstein, Inc.

Bea Feitler
Born in 1938 in Brazil · Arrived in America · Joined *Harper's Bazaar* as art director · Joined *Ms.* magazine as art director

Thomas H. Geismar
Born in 1932 · Co-founder of Chermayeff and Geismar Associates · Designed over 100 major corporate ID programs (since 1960)

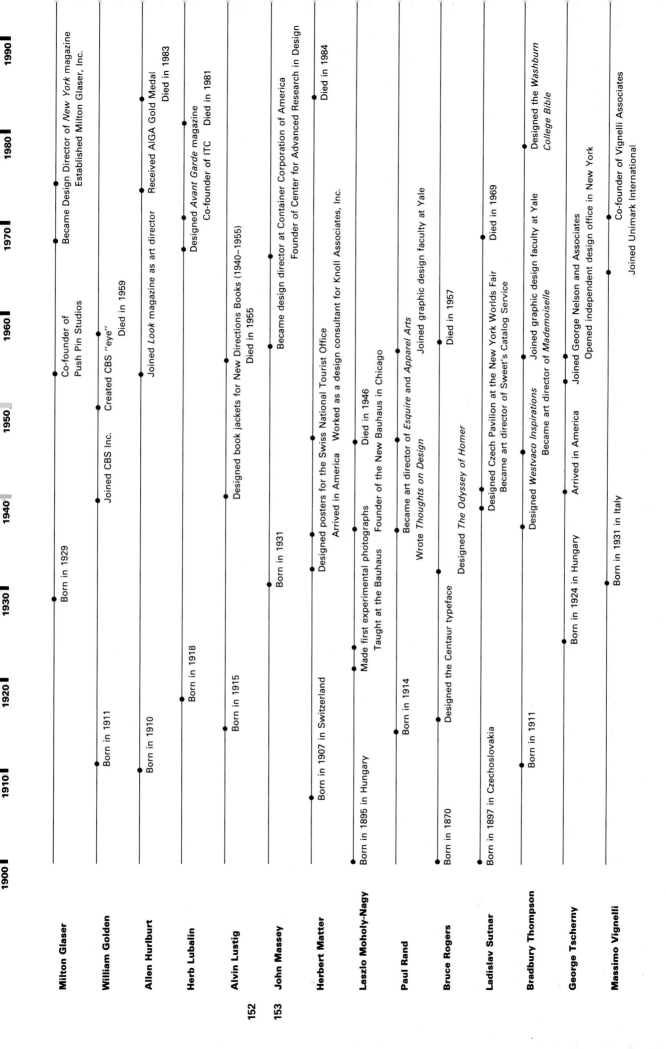

Chronology: The American Pioneers

Bibliography

Anderson, Donald M. *The Art of Written Forms.* New York: Holt, Rinehart and Winston, 1969.

Blumenthal, Joseph. *Art of the Printed Book 1455–1955.* New York: Pierpont Morgan Library, 1973.

Bojko, Szymon. *New Graphic Design in Revolutionary Russia.* New York: Praeger, 1972.

Burns, Aaron. *Typography.* New York: Van Nostrand Reinhold, 1961.

Carter, Rob, Ben Day, and Philip Meggs. *Typographic Design: Form and Communication.* New York: Van Nostrand Reinhold, 1985.

Carter, Sebastian. *Twentieth Century Type Designers.* London: Trefoil Publications Ltd., 1987.

Craig, James. *Thirty Centuries of Graphic Design.* New York: Watson-Guptill, 1987.

Dair, Carl. *Design with Type.* Toronto: University of Toronto Press, 1967.

Gardner, William. *Alphabet at Work.* New York: St. Martin's Press, 1982.

Gerstner, Karl. *Compendium for Literates: A System of Writing.* Translated by Dennis Q. Stephenson. Cambridge, MA: The MIT Press, 1974.

——. *Designing Programmes.* Teufen: Arthur Niggli AG, 1968.

Gill, Eric. *An Essay on Typography.* London: Sheed and Ward, 1931.

Goines, David Lance. *A Constructed Roman Alphabet.* Boston: David R. Godine, 1981.

Goudy, Frederic W. *The Alphabet and Elements of Lettering.* New York: Dover, 1963.

——. *Typologia: Studies in Type Design and Type-making.* Berkeley, CA: University of California, 1940.

Hurlburt, Allen. *The Grid System.* New York: Van Nostrand Reinhold, 1978.

——. *Layout: The Design of the Printed Page.* New York: Watson-Guptill, 1977.

Kelly, Rob Roy. *American Wood Type 1828–1900: Notes on the Evolution of Decorated and Large Type and Comments on Related Trades of the Period.* New York: Van Nostrand Reinhold, 1969.

Lewis, John. *The 20th Century Book: Its Illustration and Design.* 2nd ed. New York: Van Nostrand Reinhold, 1984.

——. *Typography/Basic Principles.* New York: Reinhold, 1966.

Logan, Robert K. *The Alphabet Effect: The Impact of the Phonetic Alphabet on the Development of Western Civilization.* New York: William Morrow, 1986.

Massin, Robert. *Letter and Image.* New York: Van Nostrand Reinhold, 1970.

McLean, Ruari. *Jan Tschichold: Typographer.* Boston: David R. Godine, 1975.

——. *The Thames and Hudson Manual of Typography.* London: Thames and Hudson, 1980.

Meggs, Philip B. *A History of Graphic Design.* New York: Van Nostrand Reinhold, 1983.

Morison, Stanley. *First Principles of Typography.* Cambridge: Cambridge University Press, 1936.

————, and Kenneth Day. *The Typographic Book, 1450–1935.* Chicago: The University of Chicago Press, 1964.

Muller-Brockmann, Josef. *Grid Systems in Graphic Design: A Visual Communications Manual.* Nieder-teufen, Switzerland: Arthur Niggli Ltd., 1981.

Perfect, Christopher, and Gordon Rookledge. *Rookledge's International Typefinder.* New York: PBC International, Inc., 1983.

Rand, Paul. *Thoughts on Design.* New York: Van Nostrand Reinhold, 1970.

————. *Paul Rand: A Designer's Art.* New Haven: Yale University Press, 1985.

Rogers, Bruce. *Paragraphs on Printing.* New York: Dover, 1979.

Rondthaler, Edward. *Life With Letters—As They Turned Photogenic.* New York: Hastings House, 1981.

Rosen, Ben. *Type and Typography.* New York: Van Nostrand Reinhold, 1963.

Ruder, Emil. *Typography: A Manual of Design.* Teufen AR: Arthur Niggli, 1967.

Ruegg, Ruedi. *Basic Typography.* Zurich: ABC Verlag, 1972.

Schmidt, Helmut. *Typography Today.* Tokyo: Seibundo Shin-kosha, 1980.

Solt, Mary Ellen. *Concrete Poetry: A World View.* Bloomington, IN: Indiana University Press, 1968.

Spencer, Herbert. *Pioneers of Modern Typography.* London: Lund Humphries, 1969.

————. *The Visible Word.* New York: Hastings House, 1969.

————, Editor. *The Liberated Page.* San Francisco: Bedford Press, 1987.

Sutnar, Ladislav. *Visual Design in Action—Principles, Purposes.* New York: Hastings House, 1961.

Sutton, James, and Alan Bartram. *An Atlas of Modern Typeforms.* London: Percy Lund, Humphries & Co. Ltd., 1968.

Swann, Cal. *Techniques of Typography.* New York: Watson-Guptill, 1969.

Tracy, Walter. *Letters of Credit.* London: Gordon Fraser, 1986.

Tschichold, Jan. *Treasury of Alphabets and Lettering.* Trans. by Wolf von Eckardt. Hertfordshire, England: Omega, 1985.

————. *Asymmetric Typography.* Trans. by Ruari McLean. New York: Reinhold Publishing, 1967.

————. *Designing Books.* English edition. New York: Wittenborn, Schultz, Inc., 1951.

Updike, Daniel Berkeley. *Printing Types: Their History, Forms and Use.* Cambridge, MA: Harvard University Press, 1937.

Zapf, Hermann. *Hermann Zapf and His Design Philosophy.* Chicago: STA, 1987.

————. *About Alphabets.* Cambridge: MIT Press, 1980.

————. *Typographic Variations.* New York: 1978.

————. *Manuale Typographicum.* Frankfurt and New York: Z-Presse, 1968.

Picture credits

Page 114. Josef Albers. *6 and 3,* 1931. Gouache on paper, 23 1/4 × 13 in. Hirshhorn Museum and Sculpture Garden, Smithsonian Institution. Gift of Joseph H. Hirshhorn, 1966.

Page 115. Reproduced by permission of Editions Gallimard, Paris.

Page 116 (top). Private collection.

Page 117 (bottom). Private collection.

Page 118. Max Bill. *Futurismo & Pittura Metafisica Kunsthaus Zurich,* 1950. Offset lithograph, 39 1/4 × 27 1/2 in. Collection, The Museum of Modern Art, New York. Gift of the designer.

Page 119 (top). Private collection.

Page 120 (top). A. M. Cassandre. *Chemin de Fer du Nord Nord Express,* 1927. Lithograph, 41 × 29 1/4 in. Collection, The Museum of Modern Art, New York. Gift of French National Railways.

Page 120. Courtesy of Aaron Burns.

Page 121. Courtesy of John Cage.

Page 122. Courtesy of de Harak and Poulin Associates, Inc., New York.

Page 123. Reproduced by permission of Galleria Museo Depero / VAGA New York.

Page 124. Courtesy of Douglas Higgins.

Page 125. Courtesy of Gene Federico. Photograph by Frank Cowan.

Page 126 (top). Courtesy of the Harry Ransom Humanities Research Center, University of Texas, Austin.

Page 127. Courtesy of Milton Glaser.

Page 128. Courtesy of Armin Hofmann.

Page 130. Apple LaserWriter specimens courtesy of Adobe Systems, Inc.

Page 133. Jasper Johns. *Jasper Johns Peintures & Sculptures & Dessins & Lithos,* 1960. Offset lithograph, 29 1/4 × 18 1/4 in. Collection, The Museum of Modern Art, New York. Gift of the designer.

Page 134. El Lissitzky. Proun-1 Kestnermappe (portfolio cover), 1923. Letterpress and collage on grey-green paper, 60.6 × 44.7 cm. Courtesy of The Harvard University Art Museums (Fogg Art Museum). Gift of Mr. and Mrs. Arthur E. Vershbow, Mr. and Mrs. Samuel Glaser, Mr. and Mrs. Irving W. Raab, and Mrs. Irving M. Sobin.

Page 135 (top). Reproduced by permission of the Graphic Design Archive, Rochester Institute of Technology, Rochester, New York.

Page 135. From the collection of the Herb Lubalin Study Center of Design and Typography at the Cooper Union, New York.

Page 136 (top). Kasimir Malevich. *Suprematism,* 1920. Watercolor and gouache on paper, 11 1/2 × 8 1/2 in. The Los Angeles County Museum of Art: Purchased with funds provided by Kay Sage Sanguy, Rosemary B. Baruch, and Mr. and Mrs. Charles Boyer.

Page 136. Reproduced by permission of Editions Gallimard, Paris.

Page 137. Herbert Matter. *Winterferien-Doppelte Ferien Schweiz* (Winter Vacations), 1936. Gravure, 39 3/4 × 25 1/8 in. Collection, The Museum of Modern Art, New York. Gift of G. E. Kidder Smith.

Page 138 (top). Courtesy of Josef Muller-Brockmann.

Page 138. Courtesy of Hattula Moholy-Nagy.

Page 139. Piet Mondrian. *Composition with Blue and Yellow,* 1935. Oil on Canvas, 28 3/4 × 27 1/4 in. Hirshhorn Museum and Sculpture Garden, Smithsonian Institution. Gift of Joseph H. Hirshhorn Foundation, 1972.

Page 140. Robert Rauschenberg. *Dam,* 1959. Photomechanical reproductions, cloth, and metal object on canvas, 75 1/2 × 61 5/8 in. Hirshhorn Museum and Sculpture Garden, Smithsonian Institution. Gift of Joseph H. Hirshhorn, 1966.

Page 143 (top). Courtesy of Ex Libris, New York.

Page 143. Alexander Rodchenko. Poster for "Kino Glaz," 1924. From *Rodchenko and the Arts of Revolutionary Russia,* edited by David Elliot. © 1979 by Museum of Modern Art, Oxford. Reprinted by permission of Pantheon Books, a division of Random House, Inc.

Page 144. Courtesy of Adobe Systems, Inc.

Page 145. Courtesy of Mary Ellen Solt.

Page 146. Courtesy of Ex Libris, New York.

Page 149. Courtesy of Ex Libris, New York.

Page 150. Courtesy of Wolfgang Weingart.

Page 151 (top). Courtesy of N. V. Nederlandsche Kabelfabriek.

Page 151. Courtesy of Hermann Zapf. Reproduced from *Hermann Zapf and His Design Philosophy,* STA, Chicago, 1987.

Profile portraits:

Alan Goldsmith (Armstrong)
Marie Cosindas (Casey)
Dale Quarterman (Colley)
William R. Duke (Fili)
William Rivelli (Kunz)
Jack Ramsdale (Lehrer)
Tod Gilford (Manwaring)

Index

Book design:

Rob Carter and Ben Day

Design and production assistance: John Malinoski
Production assistance: Nils Gustavsson

Typography:

Text in 11/12 Garamond #3 and 7/10 Univers 55,
set by the Linotron 202 digital typesetter.

}